Haunted
Florida

Haunted Florida

Ghosts and Strange Phenomena
of the Sunshine State

Cynthia Thuma and
Catherine Lower

Illustrations by Heather Adel Wiggins

STACKPOLE
BOOKS

Published by
STACKPOLE BOOKS
5067 Ritter Road
Mechanicsburg, PA 17055
www.stackpolebooks.com

Printed in the United States of America

10 9 8 7 6 5 4 3 2

FIRST EDITION

Cover design by Caroline Stover

Library of Congress Cataloging-in-Publication Data

Thuma, Cynthia.
    Haunted Florida : ghosts and strange phenomena of the Sunshine State / Cynthia Thuma and Catherine Lower ; illustrations by Heather Adel Wiggins. — 1st ed.
        p. cm.
    Includes bibliographical references.
    ISBN-13: 978-0-8117-3498-1 (pbk.)
    ISBN-10: 0-8117-3498-6 (pbk.)
    1. Ghosts—Florida.   2. Haunted places—Florida.   I. Lower, Catherine.   II. Wiggins, Heather Adel.   III. Title.
BF1472.U6T48   2008
133.109759—dc22

                                                            2007040121

Cynthia Thuma:
To the men in my life—Dad, Joe, Jim, and Nick—
and to Cathy Lower, a world-class coauthor
and an even better friend.

Catherine Lower:
To my mother, Lorraine Hill,
for reading to me from day one,
instilling a lifelong love of the written word.

Contents

Introduction

FLORIDA, WHOSE NAME LOOSELY TRANSLATES TO "LAND OF FLOWERS," is also known as the Sunshine State. Somehow, with the images of sunshine and the vivid hues of flowers swirling in one's consciousness at the mere mention of the state's name, it seems incongruous that ghosts and other spirits might be at work there as well. Yet they are.

From coast to coast, Florida is home to ghosts, spirits, and strange phenomena that defy conventional explanations. Whether the victims of spontaneous combustion, foul play, or just hard living, it seems that these spirits are stuck and cannot or will not move on to the next life. They haunt some of this state's most beautiful hotels and historic buildings, and they haunt some rather common places too.

Florida is a beautiful, inviting state, with white sandy beaches, swaying palm trees, coconuts, and oranges—but it also has its share of ghosts that make things go bump in the night.

North Florida

MOST PEOPLE THINK OF FLORIDA AS A PENINSULA, A DAGGER OF LAND
with a string of pearls—the Keys—attached to its end. But there
is also North Florida, which runs from the First Coast on its far
eastern edge through the Panhandle on its western side and
adheres to the underbelly of the contiguous states. This region is
the "other" Florida, a lush ribbon of land with graceful antebel-
lum homes, gently rolling hills, and vegetation such as pecan
trees and gnarly live oaks dripping with Spanish moss.

The search for the fountain of youth began in North Florida,
where Spanish conquistadores set foot on North American soil
for the first time on April 3, 1513. But the Spaniards were not the
first ones there. As early as 1000 A.D., indigenous people roamed
the area that is now North Florida. Some of the spirits encountered in North Florida today apparently come from the land's
original visitors, while others are more contemporary.

The Painted Lady

The Ancient City Inn Bed and Breakfast, also known as the Painted Lady, at 47 San Marco Avenue in St. Augustine, is a lovely bed-and-breakfast inn featuring beautiful accommodations at modest prices. A painting on one wall of the inn depicts a slightly dour woman with a fashionably long neck wearing a large, dark hat. She is the spinster daughter of the Charles Segui family, who built the home and occupied it for more than eighty years, and it seems that her ghost continues to occupy it to this day.

Over the years, she has come to be known simply as Martha Lee, a ghost as benign as her smile. Martha Lee likes fine jewelry and hats, and guests have traditionally left hats for her. Her bedroom is the most requested room in the inn.

A skeptical guest once challenged Martha Lee to prove her existence. At first nothing happened, but when he retired to his room and lay on his bed, it crashed to the floor. The inn's staff fixed the bed and tested it to determine that it was safe and sufficiently repaired. The skeptic then lay down again, and the bed crumbled once more. The staff moved him to another room, but when he stepped outside the door of the second room, it slammed shut, locking him out. The skeptic apologized to Martha Lee, and the remainder of his stay was mishap-free.

The Flagler Family Apparitions

Henry Morrison Flagler was one of the world's wealthiest men. He was accustomed to power, success, and getting what he wanted. A testament to Flagler's power and influence is that his ghost has been observed in two Florida cities. Maybe spirits—like tourists—like to go south for the winter.

Flagler's first venture, a salt-mining and production company in Michigan, ended in failure. But then he made good as a partner of John D. Rockefeller and Samuel Andrews in the Standard Oil Company. He went on his own to establish the Florida East Coast Railway.

After the death of his beloved first wife, Mary Harkness, Henry Flagler married Ida Alice Shourds, her nurse, on the rebound, but Ida turned out to be carrying lots of mental baggage. Not too long after their marriage, she began experiencing delusions, bragging about her affair with Nicholas Romanov, who had begun his reign as Czar Nicholas II the year before the Flaglers were married. She began sending the Russian monarch jewelry and expensive gifts, which Flagler's staff intercepted. Her condition grew progressively worse. For the wealthiest and most powerful entrepreneur in Florida at the turn of the century, his wife loomed as a huge liability.

Then things got more complicated. While staying with friends at one of his St. Augustine hotels in 1891, Flagler, now sixty-one, met the twenty-four-year-old Mary Lily Kenan, a stunningly beautiful young woman from Kenansville, near Wilmington, North Carolina. At first they merely bumped into each other in social circles and came to enjoy one another's company, but Henry was genuinely attracted to the vivacious Mary Lily and taking care of Ida was not a minor detail.

So he took his problem to his powerful friends in the Florida legislature, who were pleased that Flagler was bringing money and jobs to the state through the railway and the hotels he was building along the way to Key West. He urged them to pass legislation that would allow him to divorce Ida and subsequently wed Mary Lily. They complied, passing what became laughingly known as the "Flagler Divorce Bill," which permitted persons to divorce spouses with incurable mental illness of long-standing duration. The Florida media was critical, and public sentiment was overwhelmingly against him, but once freed from the albatross that was Ida, Flagler acted quickly. Two months after the law was passed, he filed for divorce. Sixty-three days later, the divorce was granted, and Henry Flagler and Mary Lily Kenan were married on August 24, 1901.

Henry Flagler presented Mary Lily with Whitehall, which was not yet complete, as her wedding gift. He told those who created Whitehall to indulge her every desire in creation of the building and its appointments. Whitehall, with fifty-five rooms covering sixty thousand square feet, was designed in the Beaux Arts style by the New York architectural firm of John Carrere and Thomas Hastings. Its interior was designed by Pottier & Stymus, also of New York.

After Henry's death, Mary Lily married Robert Worth Bingham. She died eight months later—just long enough for her to change her will and leave Bingham a very rich man, much to the consternation of her blood relatives. Bingham spent part of his inheritance to buy the *Louisville Courier-Journal* and *Louisville Times.*

Mary Lily was buried in Oakdale Cemetery in Wilmington, North Carolina, but an apparition wearing a long party dress and bearing her likeness has been observed in the hallways and a restroom at Whitehall. An apparition of Henry Flagler has also been seen at the top of the main stairway and elsewhere in the building.

Flagler College, a liberal arts college founded in 1968 in St. Augustine, occupies the former Ponce de Leon Hotel, the first of the entrepreneur's St. Augustine's hotels. Flagler later built the Alcazar, then the Cordova. The ghosts of Henry Flagler and Ida Shourds have been reported at the college's Ponce de Leon Hall. Henry's ghost apparently moved in quickly after the magnate's death. His body lay in state at the hotel's great rotunda before his funeral and interment. As the funeral party gathered to begin the procession to the Memorial Presbyterian Church, the heavy doors of the rotunda inexplicably slammed shut, momentarily stunning the mourners. Since then, an apparition resembling Henry Flagler has been observed walking the halls of the college.

A spirit resembling Ida Alice Shourds has been witnessed in the east wing of the building.

One popular ghost story about Ponce de Leon Hall is downright false, college officials insist. The tale goes that Henry kept a mistress at the hotel, on the fourth floor, and upon the woman's suicide by hanging, the floor was locked permanently. The ghost of a female seen there is said to be that of the mistress. The truth of the story is this: There was no mistress and no suicide. The fourth floor of Ponce de Leon Hall is off-limits because of concerns about its structural stability.

Henry Flagler had originally wanted to be buried in the cemetery he'd built in West Palm Beach, but after a tiff with city fathers, he decided to be buried in St. Augustine with his first wife, Mary Harkness, and Jennie, his daughter. In the afterlife, it's apparent he maintains residences in both cities.

The Henry Morrison Flagler Museum, listed on the National Register of Historic Places in 1972, is located at 1 Whitehall Way in Palm Beach. Flagler College is at 74 King Street in St. Augustine.

The Haunted Homestead Restaurant

A warm and inviting spot for hungry travelers, the Homestead Restaurant's cozy, two-story pine-log cabin building was constructed in 1934 and probably was first used as a foundling home or orphanage, then later converted into a home. It was later purchased by a radiologist, Alpha O. Paynter, who transformed it into a restaurant. She sold it in 1962 to Preben Johnson, a Jacksonville city commissioner. Johnson's daughter is the restaurant's current owner.

Ownership may have changed, but apparently Alpha still watches over the place. A variety of activities suggest she continues to be very much in charge of things. Workers say you can sometimes hear her humming as she works, turning the lights on and off, rearranging items on tables and in the kitchen.

Many ghost-hunting groups have gotten permission to conduct investigations. "They show up and start unpacking when we're cleaning up for the night," says one of the kitchen workers. During one investigation, unseen hands threw an eyeglasses case at one of the investigators.

But make no mistake, Alpha Paynter is always a polite southern lady and behaves in front of guests. As a result, the Homestead remains a popular place to eat. A combination of Low Country and tropical Florida specialties highlight the menu. The Homestead serves up heaping portions of "New Southern" cuisine to an adoring clientele. The fried chicken and fried shrimp platters are heavenly, but so are some of the newer entrées, such as Sweet Savannah sea bass oscar, Memphis-style duck confit, and pecan-dusted frenched pork chops. If those are too highfalutin, there's always fried green tomatoes, shrimp and grits, and pan-fried Georgia quail.

The Homestead Restaurant is so comfortable with its ghostly heritage that it recounts its story on the back of the menu. The part of the restaurant where the most phenomena occur is in the back, by the fireplace, and your server will happily seat you there if you ask. Perhaps Alpha Paynter will greet you personally. The restaurant is open seven days starting at 5 P.M. Sunday brunch begins at 11 A.M. The Homestead Restaurant is at 1712 Beach Boulevard in Jacksonville.

Palace Saloon's Poltergeist

Fernandina Beach, the seat of Nassau County, is on the north end of Amelia Island, not far from the Georgia border. Amelia Island is the southernmost of the Golden Isles and has long been a gathering place for the rich and famous who vacation there and at nearby Cumberland Island, Georgia. From 1880 to 1910, shipping was in its heyday, and the city's docks attracted men of lesser social standing. During those early years, the streets of the harbor district became clogged with men from all corners of the globe and stations in society. Twenty-two saloons and brothels satisfied their desires for strong drink and bawdy women.

One saloon—the Palace, known to all as "the ship captain's bar"—stood out from the rest. At 117 Centre Street, the Palace Saloon holds the distinctions of being Florida's longest continually operating bar as well as the first in the state to serve Coca-Cola.

The Beaux Arts style building originally operated as a dry-goods store and haberdashery. Louis G. Hirth bought the former Prescott Building in 1903 and gave it its present name. He called on brewer Adolphus Busch, a longtime friend, to help him design and outfit a drinking establishment without rival. Between them, they created a dignified, elegant saloon that lives on today as the shiniest jewel in the Fernandina Beach Historic District. The ceilings were lined with embossed tin, the floors covered with intricate Italian mosaics, and the walls decorated with handpainted murals. Mahogany sculptures and decorative gas lamps completed the effect.

But the beautiful appointments are not all that live on at the Palace Saloon. Locals say the spirit of a playful poltergeist nick-named Uncle Charlie pops in frequently to stir things up a little. Uncle Charlie is believed to have been an employee of the establishment who passed on to the next dimension in one of the saloon's upstairs suites.

"You can hear footsteps upstairs," says a former employee. Uncle Charlie also likes to fiddle around with the light switches and dimmers, and he's been known to admire his reflection in the mirror behind the bar.

Twice in 1999, fires broke out at the Palace Saloon, and though seriously damaged, the saloon was lovingly restored to past glory. Uncle Charlie seems to be back in his glory too.

The ex-employee recalls an early-morning event after the restoration that proved to her that Uncle Charlie hadn't abandoned the building: "I was bartending, and it was after 2 A.M., and there was one regular left in the building with me when one

of the barstools that had already been put up for the night flew off the bar. I say flew, because it landed five feet away from where it had been resting." And that wasn't quite all. "Right after it flew, the lights went dim and came back up very bright."

North Florida's Necropolis

Florida's capital city of Tallahassee has several claims to fame, primarily as home to the state's government offices and as a major education center. Located there are Florida State University, Florida A&M University, and Tallahassee Community College, which supposedly was built over an old burial ground. The city is also the necropolis of North Florida, with some graveyards and graves of particular interest.

The Old City Cemetery's most famous resident achieved little notice in life, but in death, she's been the center of speculation for decades. Elizabeth Budd Graham, Bessie to her friends, died in November 1889 at age twenty-three. Her grave, unlike the others, faces west, and the ambiguous language on the towering monument marking her final resting place leaves many suggesting she had stronger ties to the spirit world than the mortal one. Most call it the "Witch's Grave." Her inscription reads:

> Elizabeth Budd Graham, wife of John Alexander Graham, and daughter of David C. and Florence J. Wilson. Born October 19, 1866; Married November 24, 1887; Died November 16, 1889.
> A dutiful daughter, a devoted mother and a loving and faithful wife.
> Ah! Broken is the golden bowl: the spirit flown forever! Let the bell toll—a saintly soul floats on the Stygian River; Come, let the burial rite be read, the funeral song be sung; an anthem for the queenliest dead that ever died so young, a dirge for her, the doubly dead, in that she died so young.

The Old City Cemetery, ringed by Macomb Street, Call Street, Park Avenue, and Martin Luther King Boulevard, is several blocks off Tennessee Street, the city's main east-west thoroughfare. It was established in 1829 and acquired by the city in 1840. Filled with Spanish-moss-draped oak trees, the cemetery is divided into four quadrants. In the southeast section, Bessie Graham and some Confederate soldiers, largely victims of the Battles of Natural Bridge and Olustee, are interred. Black Union casualties of the Battle of Natural Bridge are interred in the southwest quadrant.

A short drive from Bessie Graham's grave, at the corner of Bronough and Brevard Streets, is Oakland Cemetery, where you'll find the graves of Sen. Claude Pepper, PGA golfer Bert Yancey, and an eccentric architect named Calvin C. Phillips. Phillips gained international acclaim for his work, including structures he designed for the 1890 World's Fair in Paris. An intelligent man, he was also odd and eccentric. He successfully combined a variety of styles in his design for the crumbling minaret-topped mausoleum where what's left of him now reposes. Just to be sure it would be an eternally fit habitat, he installed a cot and napped there regularly. Some say he's still seen occasionally at the cemetery, wandering around or sitting atop the minaret, more than eight decades after his death in 1919.

Phillips retired from his architectural practice in New York and moved to Tallahassee in 1907. His wife and two daughters chose to remain in the Empire State rather than move south. Phillips bought his plot at Oakland Cemetery the same year. As his health faltered and he knew his death was growing more imminent, he had a metal casket installed in the mausoleum. He instructed the local funeral director that upon his death, the man should alert his wife and daughters. Further, he wanted his body to be placed into the casket unembalmed, the casket to be sealed, and the mausoleum to be locked.

As the story of the eccentric architect grew, the gravesite became a popular tourist attraction, especially after sightings of Phillips began. Over the years, several break-in attempts were made, but grave robbers didn't succeed until mid-2000, when someone breached the mausoleum and removed Phillips's skull.

The Gold Coast

FLORIDA'S GOLD COAST STARTS AT ITS NORTHERNMOST BOUNDARY in Palm Beach County, runs south through Broward County, and terminates in Miami-Dade County. The region's sobriquet relates more to the value of its pricey property than to the treasure buried under its beach sand or offshore, but no matter. The three counties in the Gold Coast are a confluence of culture, climate, and lots of cash. With millionaire investors and migrant workers, Seminoles and Miccosukee Indians, voodoo and Santeria practitioners, alligators and a recent influx of feral iguanas, beings of all sorts make their homes in this area. Sometimes the mix is unusual and sometimes it's volatile—in both the mortal and spirit worlds—but most of the time people shrug off the weirdness, attributing it all to the area's location within the Bermuda Triangle, where odd things are supposed to happen and frequently do.

Anderson's General Store

Long, narrow SW 232nd Street leads through Redland, Miami-Dade County's historic agricultural district, bustling again after being hammered by Hurricane Andrew on August 24, 1992. Here, along with cornfields and groves of mango, avocado, and papaya trees laden with fruit, you'll find nurseries with exotics and ornamentals to beautify the yards of the wealthy in Kendall, Coral Gables, Key Biscayne, and beyond.

About four miles west, 232nd Street, also known as Silver Palm Drive, intersects with Newton Road, also known as SW 157th Avenue. Three of the corner properties seem in step with the times. On one corner is an orchid nursery, where unseen hands have tacked a yellow poster announcing a huge yard sale to a tree. On the northeast corner is a beautifully maintained home with a chain-link fence and a German shepherd dozing under the shade of the spreading royal poinciana tree out front. The southeast corner sports a spanking new day-care center.

But the fourth corner, the one on the southwest, harks back to the past. It is occupied by a decaying two-story building that has served variously as a general store, restaurant, rooming house, and meeting place up until Andrew's visit. A sign outside pronounces that the building is scheduled for a commercial revitalization project, but the sign, covered in green algae, looks as though it could use a little revitalization of its own.

Just to the west is an old convenience store, Anderson's Corner, where locals, many of them Hispanic agricultural workers, stop for a cold drink and hang out in the parking lot amid the pickup trucks, chatting with friends. Like the building next to it once was, it is now the social center of the Silver Palm District, named for the distinctive silver-backed palmettos that grow among the pine trees in the area. The Silver Palm Historic District is composed of the schoolhouse, built in 1904; Lions Club building, built in 1934; Kelly's Store, destroyed by Hurricane Andrew; and Anderson's General Store, built in 1912.

In 1900, William Anderson, along with Charles Gossman and Charles Hill, filed the first homestead claims in the area. Anderson was, by most accounts, a solid citizen. A Hoosier, Anderson came to West Palm Beach in 1898, moved to Jupiter, then relocated to Miami in 1900. In 1911, Anderson married Atka Harper. They divorced in 1936.

A craftsman working on a restaurant once housed in the building that is now the William Anderson General Merchandise Store, at 15700 SW 232nd Street in Goulds, described a vision he'd had of a woman as he worked there. The woman had been beaten and abused, he said. After being shown photographs of the early settlers of the area, he identified the woman as William Anderson's stepdaughter, and Anderson as the abuser. The craftsman also said he heard knocking and bumping noises in the building. A family who lived in the building reported hearing the sounds of a young girl's and man's voices screaming, banging, and chains being dragged through the vacant upstairs, as well as lights being turned on and off in the upstairs areas. Is the spirit of Anderson's stepdaughter still desperately trying to get away from her abuser?

The Phantoms of Biltmore Hotel

If, as a growing film location, South Florida ever needs a castle for a film, the Biltmore Hotel, at 1200 Anastasia Avenue in Coral Gables, would serve the purpose well. Like a tiara for the City Beautiful, the majestic hotel grows out of the land once occupied by a humble tomato field, a perfect example of architectural alchemy executed by the partnership of Schulze and Weaver of New York, who designed a significant portion of South Florida's landmark architecture. Palm Beach's Breakers hotel, the Miami Freedom Tower, and Miami's Ingraham Building, all now listed on the National Register of Historic Places, are Schulze and Weaver designs.

The grand hotel was the dream of Coral Gables founder George Merrick and Biltmore Hotels patriarch John McEntee Bowman. Construction began on Friday, February 13, 1925. It rises to fifteen stories in its magnificent central tower, designed to resemble the Giralda Tower in Seville, Spain. The tower is flanked by a pair of ten-story wings that are, in turn, flanked by seven-story wings. The visual impact of the exterior is stunning, but the interior is even more so. The Biltmore Hotel boasts of 280 luxurious rooms and nearly as many ghosts. What more would one expect from a place that started construction on Friday the thirteenth?

When the hotel opened on January 14, 1926, the $10 million edifice featured typical activities such as swimming in the 22,000-square-foot pool, the largest in the continental United States, and playing golf on two eighteen-hole championship courses, as well as more exotic pursuits such as polo, fox hunting, or gliding in one of twenty-six gondolas imported from Venice. The hurricane later that year created the first of many huge bumps in the road for the hotel, destroying much of the area and effectively ending tourism for a while.

The Biltmore's ghostly history got its start during the hotel's early heyday, when Thomas "Fatty" Walsh, a corpulent, unctuous thug who operated a high-stakes casino on the thirteenth floor of the tower, was gunned down by a rival. As Walsh lay bleeding on the expensive carpeting, his assailant was spirited out. Today Walsh apparently is the leader of an unruly pack of spirits who reveal themselves in a variety of ways at the hotel. Fatty Walsh's favorite activity seems to be fiddling with the elevators and the lights. There is supposed to be limited access to the infamous thirteenth floor, but whenever Fatty's in the mood, folks say, he stops the elevator there capriciously.

Through the start of World War II, the Biltmore functioned as Dade County's grandest hotel, where politicians, financiers, and celebrities were sure to stay if visiting the area. The war changed all that, transforming the grand building into a cavernous Veterans Administration hospital, with gray linoleum covering the beautiful marble floors and thick layers of dull paint on the walls.

The hotel remained a VA facility until 1968, when it was closed. Another period of ghostly activity seems to have begun at that time, when the great hotel lay empty and spirits played pranks on security officers and Coral Gables police.

In 1973, the City Beautiful was granted ownership of the hotel, but for the next decade, it remained shuttered. Finally, in 1983, retrofitting and renovations began in an effort to return the hotel to its former glory. After four years of work and nearly $55 million, the great hotel opened again on December 31, 1987.

Apparently Fatty Walsh is back in all his glory, too, as are other ghosts who occasionally show up inside and outside the hotel, in the rooms, ballrooms, and other common areas. The accommodations and the dining have never been better. Nor, for that matter, have the many happy haunts of the Biltmore.

The Biltmore spirits are a recognized part of the hotel's ambience. The hotel offers ghost stories around the great fireplace in the lobby weekly.

British Bertha of the Blue Anchor

Bertha still shares her anguish at her transplanted home

Less than a block from the Intracoastal Waterway and a few blocks from Delray Beach's world-famous public beach, the Blue Anchor Pub sits quietly on the south side of chichi Atlantic Avenue. Had the exterior of the pub not been lovingly disassembled and shipped to South Florida, it would undoubtedly be easier to overlook. With its somber dark wood and stained-glass windows, it seems an anomaly amid the airy, tropical colors along the avenue.

The Blue Anchor, now at 804 E. Atlantic Avenue in Palm Beach County's Delray Beach, originally stood on Chancery Lane in London. Two of its female patrons, Elizabeth "Long Liz"

Gustafsdottir Stride and Catherine "Kate" Eddows, both age forty-four when they died, are believed to have spent their last evening of life at the Blue Anchor in 1888. Whether they met Jack the Ripper at the pub or later in the streets is unclear. Saucy Jacky, as the Ripper referred to himself, apparently met most of his five victims in pubs. He met victims Annie Chapman and Marie Jeanette "Mary Jane" Kelly at another London pub, the Ten Bells.

The ghosts of Kate and Long Liz have yet to appear at the Blue Anchor, but the apparition of an unfaithful wife, Bertha Starkey, has. Bertha was fatally stabbed in the pub by her enraged husband after he returned from sea and found her in the clutches of her paramour there. The ghost of Bertha apparently made the trip across the Atlantic with the building's facade and makes occasional appearances. She's been known to bleat a plaintive wail every now and then in the quiet hours after the pub has closed and staff is cleaning up. Others have reported hearing her footsteps pacing upstairs, even though the Blue Anchor is a one-story building.

Bertha's behavior has unsettled staff, set off burglar alarms and motion detectors, and tantalized ghost-hunting groups. To keep her at bay, staff members ring a bell and chant a little hymn at 10 P.M. nightly, the hour she was murdered. Doing so seems to help keep Bertha placated, for the most part.

Like the atmosphere, the food at the Blue Anchor is very British, right down to the beloved mushy peas. For people whose souls are made whole by a plate of bangers and mash or bubble 'n' squeak, the Blue Anchor is an oasis; for those more haughty about haute cuisine or libations, the bar serves all the usual bubbly imports, as well as Boddingtons, Smithwick's, and Newcastle Brown. The atmosphere is authentic and inviting, and the staff friendly and efficient too.

The Mysteries of Boca Raton

When Addison Mizner was a boy growing up in Benicia, California, one of the places he and his younger brother Wilson enjoyed playing was the twenty-four-acre city cemetery, which overlooked the city and the Carquinez Straits. Earthquakes had caused some of the gravestones to topple, and the winds that whipped along the straits and pounding rains further damaged the terrain, giving the cemetery a ramshackle, spooky appearance. The highest point in the graveyard was the obelisk atop the grave of Mary Lynch, a local schoolteacher. The Mizner boys holed up at the cemetery and made up ghost stories to scare the wits out of their younger cousins and the younger children in town, keeping them away from their favorite play place. When Mizner moved east to Florida and became a famous society architect, he learned of another ghost tale at the hotel he designed, built, and helped operate. Or did he make this story up as well?

Mizner built the Cloister Inn in 1926 and opened it as the most luxurious resort on the planet. The inn had a hundred rooms and cost $1.25 million to build. Mizner was more than just the resort's financier and architect; he also designed the gardens and selected the plants, and he even designed the interior furnishings such as tissue boxes and ashtrays. Mizner Development Corporation and Mizner Industries, which he also owned, made the architectural features, including terra cotta barrel roof tiles, architectural trim, lanterns, and wrought-iron work. Unlike the buildings he designed for the rich and famous, the Cloister Inn was something very special for Addison Mizner, and he wanted it to operate flawlessly.

Advertising for the southernmost city in Palm Beach County boasted, "I am the grandest resort in the world. I am Boca Raton." Addison and brother Wilson used their connections in society, industry, and entertainment to attract the world's upper crust as clientele. They knew that the area's beauty, the inn's appointments, and the staff's efficiency would bring them back.

One of the best chambermaids, whom Mizner reportedly assigned to special or hard-to-please guests, was Esmeralda, who was otherworldly when it came to anticipating their needs. It is said that Esmeralda died in a fire but returns to the resort frequently to make sure all remains in order. She turns off lights, tidies up the freshly cut flowers, and takes care of small details that even the best house staff members sometimes overlook. Always the perfectionist, Esmeralda still takes care of all the little touches. Every hotel should have at least one ghost like her.

But did Esmeralda ever really exist? Addison Mizner's family biography, *The Many Mizners,* exaggerates the truth in parts. To stimulate sale of Boca Raton land, Addison and Wilson buried some Spanish gold pieces on their Boca Raton property and arranged for their discovery, which was well covered by the media. Addison Mizner had on his staff a public-relations genius named Harry Reichenbach, who wasn't above a little supernatural hocus-pocus, especially if it generated publicity and brought in more guests.

The area around the inn, now known as the Boca Raton Resort and Club, at 501 E. Camino Real, has been the scene of many tales of otherworldly phenomena over the years. During the city's early days, square-masted sailing vessels were reportedly seen in Lake Boca Raton, which adjoins the hotel, yet the opening to Lake Boca Raton is far too shallow to allow boats that large to enter.

Just south of the resort and club is the Boca Raton inlet, which provides access to Lake Boca Raton from the ocean. In the 1920s or so, on the inlet's south shore, a large gumbo-limbo tree grew amid a dense hammock. Somewhere under the great tree, local legend held, lay the buried booty of a pirate who plied the warm waters of South Florida. After the pirate's death, whenever people ventured into the jungle, a large white gull would appear seemingly from nowhere, screeching, circling, and diving at the trespassers. After a few years, the gull—believed to be the ghost of the pirate—disappeared.

Also in the 1920s, a light was visible off the Boca Raton public beach near the resort and club. The area from which the light seemed to appear was over a rocky reef where sailing ships had earlier been lured ashore by buccaneers, who lit bonfires to lure them, then looted and plundered their ships. Folks who walked along the beach in the direction of the light found that when they got as close as possible to the source of the light, it disappeared, but if they retraced their steps to about a quarter mile away, the light appeared again. The light disappeared for good after the 1928 hurricane.

Many questions remain unanswered about the Boca Raton Resort and Club and the area surrounding it. Unless Esmeralda herself appears to straighten out the confusion, we may never know the whole truth. Perhaps she can explain everything

Chupacabras

Perhaps they came east from the Everglades, but they're out there, believers insist. They wait silently in the dark for the moment you open your door to let your dog or cat out at night. When you're back in the house, they strike silently and swiftly. They'll dine on your dogs, chomp on your chickens, and they're guaranteed to get your goat.

Those who scoff at the possibility that chupacabras actually exist laughingly refer to them as Latin leprechauns. The name, translated from Spanish, means "goat sucker." Those few who report having seen them describe small, vicious mammals with intense red eyes—creatures that can cause carnage, terror, and destruction in amounts far greater than their physical stature. They are reputed to wait for just the right moment to attack so that they can savagely overcome their stunned prey, puncture its neck with their fangs, and leave behind a drained carcass with a telltale pair of perfectly matched puncture wounds.

Few say they have actually witnessed chupacabras, but many have reportedly seen the carnage left in their wake—goats, dogs,

cats, smaller prey such as chickens and ducks, and even the occasional cow or two—all left horrendously mutilated and drained of their blood.

Although many fear the chupacabras, or chupas for short, skeptics insist that they are the product of idle minds. Yet local practitioners of Santeria, who have been known to ritually slaughter animals as part of their religion's rites, have blamed the chupas for the animal carcasses that sometimes litter Miami-Dade County, particularly the community of Sweetwater, which seems to be ground zero for chupa activity.

If a police sketch artist were to create a picture of this nocturnal predator, the portrait would be a grotesque one. Eyewitness accounts vary somewhat, but in general, from their descriptions, chupacabras resemble kangaroos that may have lived under high-voltage lines too long. They are gray in color and possess a phenomenal jumping ability. Unlike kangaroos, a row of razor-sharp quills protrudes from the spine. The chupa also has glowing red eyes, a long pointed tongue, and fangs. The armlike upper appendages are webbed, which enhances the creature's jumping ability.

The first documented chupacabra attack took place in Canovanas, Puerto Rico, in December 1994. Since then, they have left a trail of blood and entrails in Mexico, the Dominican Republic, Chile, Costa Rica, and the United States. The greatest amount of chupa activity reported in the United States is in Miami-Dade County, but their American trail of death and destruction extends to Texas, California, New York, New Jersey, and Massachusetts.

There are few reports of chupa attacks outside Hispanic neighborhoods, and Hispanic children are routinely chastised by their parents for telling their younger siblings that chupas will get them. Others are likely to chalk up random animal deaths to packs of feral dogs, coyotes . . . or vampires.

The Clammy Commission Chamber

Wilton Manors, located just north of Fort Lauderdale, is a small city accustomed to doing things its own way. In 1956, the city acquired a piece of land from Food Fair on which to build a municipal complex. Architect William Bigoney designed a compact municipal complex containing the normal amenities, as well as headquarters for the fire and police departments, including several holding cells. Construction started later that year.

The fire department moved to a more spacious building three blocks away in June 1969, and the two truck bays were converted into larger chambers for the city commission. But the room there is just a bit odd.

It's not just during the city commission meetings when things grow a mite icy in the room. City employees who find they need to work alone or late at night in City Hall go to all lengths to avoid going into the council chamber. "I used to lock the door between the hallway and the council chamber," says one city employee who asked not to be identified. "It's in the commission chamber where everybody notices things."

City Hall workers and cleaning staff say that the room has cold spots and they feel as though they are being watched by unseen eyes. Others say they occasionally feel a subtle warm breath down the backs of their collars or catch a glimpse of someone darting out of sight. When they muster the courage to pursue, they find no one there.

How long the cold spots and the other manifestations remain will be difficult to tell. Plans were underway as of 2007 to raze the City Hall complex, at 524 NE 21st Court, and build a new one.

Coral Castle

Like many whose love life ended in a puddle of tears and a heap of dashed dreams, Edward Leedskalnin needed to clear his head and opted for a change of scenery when the love of his life, his fiancee Agnes Scuffs, dumped him like a pair of old socks. He was twenty-six at the time; she was sixteen and thought Leedskalnin was too old, far too weird, and much too poor for her tastes. He had thought she was a temple of purity, his "Sweet Sixteen." Her rejection on the eve of their wedding left him stunned. He severed all ties to his native Latvia and cast himself adrift in North America.

After bouncing around Canada and the northern United States, he wandered south until he found himself in Florida City, ten miles south of Homestead in Miami-Dade County. He wound up in the midst of South Dade's farming area, in a spot that was little more than a dot on the map. The rich South Dade soil yields an incredible bounty—mangoes, papayas, key limes, avocados, corn, peppers, eggplant, beans, greens, and more—but Leedskalnin coaxed something else from the ground: coral, South Florida's bedrock. Working alone with pulleys, sleds, blocks, tackles, and other tools he made himself, Leedskalnin cut and transported huge blocks of coral to his property, where he built a park dedicated to the lost love of his life.

Leedskalnin was an eccentric man of five feet, a hundred pounds, whose idea of an evening of fun was experimenting with magnetic current or writing about his theories on the subject. He wrote and self-published three booklets on the subject of magnetism. He also produced a booklet titled *Mineral, Vegetable and Animal Life* and a strange, rambling treatise on love, life, and the sexes called *A Book in Every Home.* He left every other page blank so that the reader could write his or her dissenting opinions on them.

He ordinarily lived on a diet of cereal and bananas, but when he was feeling really adventuresome, Leedskalnin splurged, eating sardines and peppers for a change of pace. In 1923, he set about creating Rock Gate Park on an acre of land he'd purchased for $12, working alone at night by the light of a single lantern, using primitive tools he had made by hand or scavenged from junkyards. He achieved stunning results that still have engineers and geologists scratching their heads. Rock Gate Park became Florida's Stonehenge, a shrine to the gods, a place to pray and reflect, and a tribute to Leedskalnin's love of the elements and search for purity and perfection.

"A normal male is always ready to strive for perfection, the female is not," he wrote in *A Book in Every Home*. But Leedskalnin was clearly no normal male. How did he move a total of more than 1,000 tons of coral in the walls and another 1,000 tons in furnishings of the sculpture garden, most of it in huge blocks that weigh thousands of pounds each? Coral is a finicky and porous substance that is difficult to work with. It weighs 125 pounds per cubic foot, but Leedskalnin found a way to master it. He was sinewy and strong for his size and weight, but certainly not Superman. Some said he was able to summon otherworldly forces to assist him in his labor. Did some superhuman force help Odd Eddie move all those big rocks?

In 1937, when Rock Gate Park's serenity was threatened by a housing development creeping toward it, Leedskalnin packed it up and, with the aid of a friend with a tractor, moved it north to ten acres in Homestead, its current home. The new park, the Coral Castle, was more than Leedskalnin's greatest achievement—it was also his home. He trudged the sixteen steps to the top of the two-story tower to his tiny bedroom, where he slept on a bed made of discarded planks wrapped in burlap and suspended from the ceiling.

The sculpture garden is a tribute to Leedskalnin's knowledge of astronomy, physics, and geology. He also showed he was a craftsman, filling the spaces between the giant blocks of coral with small stones to make a seamless fit. He dug a spring-fed well and carved a bathtub. His cooking station was a forerunner of the pit barbecue. His telescope focuses perfectly on the North Star. The Throne Room contains thrones for himself, his Sweet Sixteen, and a child. Behind the thrones are heavenly bodies carved from coral—Mars, Saturn, a crescent moon, and a smaller crescent.

Leedskalnin charged 10 cents for admission to the park. If he was in the mood, he'd welcome his guests and guide them through the park and demonstrate how the features functioned. If not, he simply ignored them.

In December 1951, Leedskalnin felt very ill. He tacked a note to the door of the castle that he was going to the hospital. He locked the gate and boarded a bus to Jackson Memorial Hospital in Miami, where he was diagnosed with stomach cancer. He died three days later in his sleep at age sixty-four. Leedskalnin is buried in Miami Memorial Park, a few miles north of Homestead. He rests under an oak tree beneath a granite headstone that notes: "Born in Latvia. Creator of Coral Castle." A few orchids are carved into his headstone, reminiscent of the orchids that grow at his castle even today.

Edward Leedskalnin was certainly eccentric and believed he would live forever, and perhaps he does. Coral Castle, at 28655 South Dixie Highway, remains a favorite meeting spot for psychic and Renaissance fairs. Psychics who visit there say they often feel a strong presence in the castle, particularly in Ed's room.

Magnetism always was his strong suit.

The Lost Patrol

It was supposed to be a routine training mission, but it was nothing of the sort.

The weather was good on December 5, 1945, when a squadron of five TBM Avenger aircraft took off from the Fort Lauderdale Naval Air Station on a training flight. Ninety minutes into the mission, one of the planes radioed the tower, reporting that the pilots could no longer see the land and were off course.

Thirty minutes later, another transmission crackled over the radio, confirming that the squadron was completely lost.

Completely lost. Those were the last two words heard from them.

Four of the pilots were novices who were flying by the seats of their pants. The compass in the lead plane was broken; none of the planes had clocks. In the six decades since their disappearance, dozens of World War II military aircraft have been plucked from the sea, as well as the Everglades and other swamplands throughout southeastern Florida, but no traces of the Lost Patrol planes or the fifteen crewmembers were ever found.

The Lost Patrol is the best-known story used to give credence to the theory of the Bermuda Triangle, also called the Devil's Triangle, where planes and ships seem to vanish without a trace of evidence or scrap of debris. Within this area, located by drawing a line on the map from Bermuda to Puerto Rico and then another to southeastern Florida, strange forces seem to be at work, swallowing up ships, planes, and people.

A variety of theories have been offered to explain the disappearance of the Lost Patrol and other craft and people in the Bermuda Triangle. A strong magnetic field, sea creatures of gigantic proportion, and other causes all have been blamed. Since the mid-1970s, however, interest in the Bermuda Triangle has waned, particularly as South Florida and the Bahamas have blossomed as tourist destinations with heavy air, ship, and pleasure-boat travel.

Riddle House at Yesteryear Village

Snuggled near the center of the sprawling, dusty South Florida Fairgrounds at 9067 Southern Boulevard in West Palm Beach's wild, wild west lies Yesteryear Village, a small burg brimming with Florida history. Begun in 1990 as a way of preserving the history of South Florida, Yesteryear Village has grown swiftly, but nearly silently, and now boasts a variety of buildings, including a bait-and-tackle store, schoolhouse, church, general store, several museums, hunter's shack, fire station, the entrance gates from the town of Golfview, and even its own haunted house.

The haunted house is one with historic value, the home of West Palm Beach's first city manager, Karl Riddle. The house, built in 1904–05, originally was located at 327 Acacia Road, across from Woodlawn Cemetery downtown, and served as home to the cemetery's caretaker. Riddle lived there from 1920 to 1923. After his departure, it was transformed to City House, used to provide temporary housing for new city employees and their families. Much later, in the 1980s, it became the property of Palm Beach Atlantic University, which first used the building as a small dormitory. When the college planned to raze the building, Yesteryear Village asked for it.

Not long after Riddle House was relocated at Yesteryear Village, guests began reporting unusual occurrences. Some claimed they saw heads looking out of the attic, which is off-limits to visitors, but one woman, who asked that her name not be used, had an entirely different experience: "My son, our guide, and I had gone inside the home, and we'd walked upstairs to the bedroom at the top of the stairs. My son was transfixed at the sight of the antique toys, particularly the antique train sets in the upstairs bedroom. As we stood, I heard the string of bells on the front door ring. The door opened, then closed. I was at the top of the steps and looked down when the bells rang. I watched as it opened, then closed just as gently as our guide had closed it earlier, but no one had entered that I could see. I don't believe in ghosts, but I have to admit, I'm spooked over that. Maybe my surprise showed on my face, but the guide didn't miss a beat. 'It's probably just the ghost,' she said with a shrug. She wasn't kidding. She was very matter-of-fact about it."

Snake Warrior's Island

Snake Warrior's Island was once considered to be on the eastern border of the Everglades, but the westward march of civilization has consumed much of the wetlands. Named for the Seminole chief Chitto Tustenuggee, who lived in the area in the mid-1880s, what once was a swampy island is now a fifty-three-acre county-owned park in the midst of a subdivision just to the north side of the Miami-Dade–Broward County line.

At the turn of the twentieth century, and for more than twenty years thereafter, a variety of strange lights and apparitions originating from the island were reported. Orbs, some as big as beach balls and others as bright as yellow tennis balls, were seen rising like bubbles from the island and floating heavenward, accompanied by wailing. The unnatural glow shimmered in the night sky, and the humming sound that accompanied them beckoned farmers who lived in the area. When the curious locals crept onto the island to get a better look, the lights and sounds disappeared.

Formerly a reserve parcel, the state-owned land is now a nature park, opened to the public in January 2004. The park is slated to undergo further development, including restrooms, a welcome center, and a covered shelter. It is a block north of the intersection of County Line Road and NW 62nd Avenue in Miramar.

Theaters with a Great Boo

It seems that the most haunted commercial properties throughout Florida are theaters. These are not the kind of theaters where films are shown, but the ones where live performances take place. There's apparently something spirits find irresistible there. Perhaps it's all that energy.

Palm Beach County is a lively community of the arts and serves as home to two cozy playhouses, in Lake Worth and Delray Beach, that reputedly have become home to guests who have answered life's final curtain.

Lake Worth Playhouse is as neat as a bandbox, perfectly situated at 713 Lake Avenue. It's not déjà vu if you feel you've seen the area before. The 1981 noir thriller *Body Heat,* featuring William Hurt and Kathleen Turner, was filmed there. The shops along Lake Avenue are mostly owned by individuals or families, giving the downtown a real hometown feel.

Brothers Lucien E. and Clarence E. Oakley opened the Oakley Theater in 1924 in a restored vaudeville theater that still had its original pecky cypress ceiling. The little theater suffered through some tough times, first bashed by the September 17 category four hurricane of 1926, then slammed by the great hurricane of 1928. The big storm killed 1,836 and injured 1,870. The stock market crashed in 1929. Lucien Oakley could only take so much. In 1931, he shot himself.

After his death, strange palmprints appeared on the theater's walls. Cold spots develop in parts of the theater and disappear just as quickly. Doors slam shut without apparent reason, and footsteps have been heard onstage when the stage is empty. Staff members say that when Lucien Oakley likes the play, he's a hands-off kind of ghost. When he disapproves, he shows his displeasure.

Delray Beach Playhouse is located at 950 NW Ninth Street, in a comfortable residential neighborhood on the south shore of Lake Ida, a haven for water-ski enthusiasts. The playhouse got its start in 1946 in the parish hall of St. Paul's Church, then relocated to the building now occupied by the city library before moving to its present cozy, 238-seat location.

From the start, establishing the theater company and a theatrical tradition in the city has been a struggle, but Bob Blake, one of the theater's founders, was always there to help. An architect, he designed the playhouse building more than four decades ago. Some say he's still there keeping watch over it. An apparition resembling him was seen on the stage late one night, and he has been heard opening and closing doors throughout the building.

Both playhouses offer an impressive selection of performances and embrace their ghostly tradition. Clearly, both ghosts have their theaters' best interests in mind.

Paranormal Phenomena at Tropication Arts

A huge, dark cloud rolls west from the Everglades toward the ocean, racing to outrun the approaching darkness on a midsummer Friday evening. Most on NE 54th Street in Miami's Little Haiti pay little heed. The mood on the street is festive, and the milder temperatures caused by the approaching storm bring a welcome relief. The boom box propped in the window of a record shop blasts a steady stream of up-tempo island music, and the scent of fish frying wafts on the breeze. Workers returning home make light, animated conversation as they encounter friends and neighbors along the way.

A Haitian radio station whose offices are at 117 NE 54th Street is dark and quiet. The windows are tightly shut, and no friends linger in conversation outside. In the same block of shops, a botanica is several shops to the right, at the corner. Several stores to the left is another botanica, which offers "occult sciences" supplies among other things. In a community that has come to embrace Santeria, Orisha, Palo Mayombe, and voodoo to varying degrees, spirituality is a strong and pervasive force. The still, silent shop at number 117 seems protected by spirits. Or is it protected from them?

In 1967, things were hardly quiet there. The building was a warehouse known as Tropication Arts, purveyors of tasteful to tacky Florida souvenirs, lagniappe, and other gimcracks. The wholesaler kept gift shops, five-and-ten stores, and sundries shops well stocked with salt-and-pepper shakers, spoon rests, shot glasses, and ceramic ashtrays from Hong Kong in the shapes of oranges, flamingos, and palm trees. Whether one euphemistically called it Floridiana or kitsch, Tropication Arts carried it.

Items were flying off the shelves at Tropication Arts, but it wasn't because business was so brisk. Rather, the hiring of a nineteen-year-old shipping clerk named Julio seemed to trigger an onslaught of unexplainable activity, with items rolling off tables and smashing into walls, though some believed the occurrences were caused by restless spirits. Police looked into the phenomena. Academics asked questions. Paranormal researchers made inquiries and suggested that an exorcism might put an end to the weirdness, but Julio refused.

Some time after the phenomena began, the building was burglarized, and Julio was accused. Police said he confessed, but he and the shop's owner said he didn't.

After Tropication Arts, Julio went to work for a shoe store, then a sundries store. Both stores experienced phenomena similar to that which occurred at Tropication Arts.

Julio eventually got married and fathered a beautiful daughter. Several weeks after the child's birth, he was held at gunpoint at his job at an automobile service station. He was shot twice, including once to the heart, but he survived. A group of researchers interested in parapsychology and psychokinesis offered to pay him to become a research subject, but he refused. He'd grown weary of the weirdness and attention and didn't want it to continue.

The Lady of Villa Paula

The homes that line busy North Miami Avenue in Little Haiti are largely post–World War II starter homes, built in the open, patio style common to South Florida, but decorated in the manner of the homeland of their newest owners, who have dressed them in colors not otherwise seen in South Florida. Bright, splashy colors are hardly rare in Miami-Dade County, from the signature flamingo, teal, emerald, and coral of *Miami Vice* to the peach, lemon, mauve, turquoise, and azure tones commonly seen on South Beach, but the colors and their combinations in Little Haiti are unique. Across the street and not far from a lavender house with yellow ochre roof and trim is a building that seems stodgy and curiously out of step with the architecture and decor of the neighborhood. An iron and cement fence reinforced by many years' growth of dense bougainvillea and air potatoes forms a thick barrier and serves to further discourage visitors. With its flat roof, formal Neoclassical design, and lavish tile work fading in the sun, Villa Paula stands out like a big, whitewashed thumb.

Located at 5811 N. Miami Avenue, Villa Paula, which for four years housed the Cuban consulate in the United States, was designed by a Havana architect named Freira and built in 1925 by Cuban workers. It is the only building in Miami known to be constructed by the Cuban government. The ten-room edifice with a separate gazebo and garage served as home and headquarters for Don Domingo Milord, the consul, and his wife, Paula. The Milords lived and entertained in the graceful building featuring thirteen-foot ceilings, Tuscan columns, and yellow brick sent from Cuba. But the mistress of the mansion died four years later, succumbing to complications from surgery to amputate her leg. Some who are familiar with the grand old house and the neighborhood say that the lady of the house, embittered and vengeful, lived there long after 1929.

Helen Reardon purchased the building in 1960 and lived there for the next thirty years. After that it became a group home for senior citizens. A later owner restored the villa to its former grandeur, refurbishing the beautiful mahogany doors and stained-glass windows and filling it with period antiques. He hoped to transform it into an upscale restaurant, museum, or Cuban cultural center that could have connected to Lemon City Park or Toussaint L'Overture Elementary School, which are both behind the building, but the changing demographics of the neighborhood made doing so impossible. It now serves as a medical office and is a Miami-Dade County historical landmark. It is not open to the public.

The apparition of a woman gliding through the building in party attire has been reported. Villa Paula seems to be a center for other unexplained supernatural activity as well, from small things such as the sound of classical music and the aroma of cigar smoke and strong Cuban coffee wafting from the building to darker and more sinister occurrences such as the discovery of dead animals on the property. Visitors and residents said doors mysteriously slammed on windless nights. Knocking sounds came incessantly from the front door, but when the door was opened, no one was outside. Psychics reported that they sensed a dark, malevolent presence brooding. Since the mid-1990s, however, the apparitions have ceased, and Dona Paula Milord, like most of her Cuban countrymen, seems to have abandoned the neighborhood.

The Florida Keys

THE FLORIDA KEYS, THE DELICATE STRING OF CORAL "PEARLS" OFF the southern tip of the Florida mainland, are a place like none other. They are a great place to get away, and as many have found throughout the years, the Keys are also a superb place to hide away.

In the part of Florida where the sun may shine a bit brighter, the Keys are known for the laid-back, live-and-let-live demeanor of their residents. But human behavior in Florida's southernmost county might be a bit more aberrant, and sometimes it can grow very bizarre indeed.

The Strange Love Affair of Karl Tanzler

Karl Tanzler, like many others, came to Florida to reinvent himself. He seemed to enjoy blurring the lines between fiction and nonfiction in his life. Born in January or February of 1877, Georg Karl Tanzler dubbed himself Count Carl von Cosel, and other names, but in Key West, few cared.

Karl Tanzler had first seen Elena Milagro Hoyos Mesa as an apparition when he was twelve, decades before her birth. He spent much of his life hounded by the vision and searched for the petite, raven-haired beauty in the white dress in Europe, Australia, and the United States. When he least expected to find her, he finally did, while working as an X-ray technologist in Key West's Marine Hospital.

One April day in 1930, Elena Hoyos walked into his life for a blood test and an X-ray. Her family, from Cuba, had fallen on hard times, and her own young life had just taken a hard turn for the worse. Only weeks earlier, things had seemed so promising. She and her husband, Luis Mesa, were expecting their first child. But in the eighth month, she became ill and miscarried. When she continued to feel weak and ill, her doctor prescribed some tests, and the diagnosis was shocking—tuberculosis. Not long thereafter, Luis bolted for another woman. Elena's hopes of becoming a mother were dashed, her marriage failed, and her health was deteriorating, but her supportive yet struggling family was still there for her.

By the time Elena met Karl Tanzler, whose X-rays would confirm the diagnosis and show the advanced stage of her disease, she was in deep despair. She was touched by the kindness and attention that the older man with the German accent and the Vandyke beard lavished upon her. Clearly she was not just another patient to him.

For his part, Tanzler could barely contain his enthusiasm. He had found the woman with the dainty hands, porcelain-colored skin, mysterious eyes, and pouty lips whose image had long tantalized and tortured him at night. He could barely concentrate as he performed the tests.

Tanzler was fifty-three and Hoyos twenty-one when they met. A native of Dresden, Germany, Karl boasted of regal bloodlines and degrees from nine German universities. In postwar Key West, he was happy to find work as a hospital technician and was well respected for his work even if he wasn't very well liked. He was tall, thin, and spindly, and his formality and imperiousness didn't make him a good fit with his laid-back colleagues.

The tests confirmed that Elena's tuberculosis was advanced and her time was limited. Tanzler immediately ingratiated himself with her and her family. He offered to come to their home and treat her for free. The grateful relatives accepted. Despite his ministrations, Elena's condition worsened quickly. He proposed marriage, but she turned him down. She succumbed to her disease on October 25, 1931. Tanzler offered to pay for Elena's funeral, mausoleum, and headstone. He also wanted to buy her bed and rent her room at the Hoyos's home. The cash-strapped family agreed. Tanzler instructed the funeral director at Lopez Funeral Home that Elena's body was not to be embalmed.

Months passed. Tanzler moved out of the Hoyos household and into a place of his own, where he could keep the shell of a wingless airplane he had purchased. Each night, he'd walk to visit the cemetery, where he'd unlock the door to the mausoleum for a chat with his beloved. He sometimes brought a radio along to play music for her.

He looked and played the part of the grieving lover, but it was all an act. The body of Elena Hoyos was not in the grave bearing her name, and Karl Tanzler knew it. He had already removed her body from the mausoleum.

It had happened during the cover of darkness one night in 1933. Tanzler put his plan into action during his regular nocturnal

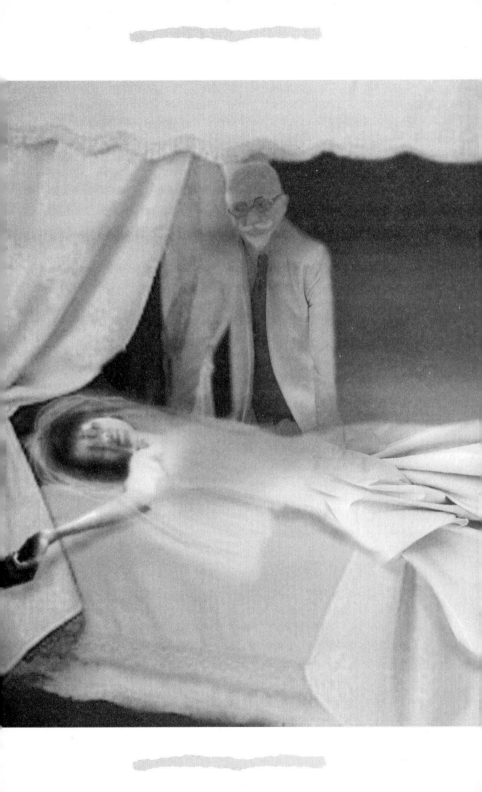

visit. He loaded Elena's decomposing remains into a wheelbarrow and carted them off to his home, where he lovingly carried her into the fuselage of the wingless airplane. His plan was to restore her to life, fix the plane, and fly off to heaven with her. On the nose of the plane, he painted, "Countess Elaine von Cosel."

Tanzler worked diligently on minimizing the effects of decomposition. He bathed the remains with strong disinfectants, stripped away decayed flesh, and replaced it with wax or plaster, covered with silk. He carefully wired her joints when the connective tissue lost its elasticity.

He moved her remains into the bedroom of his home, talked to her, sang love songs to her, and played them on his tiny handmade organ. He was particularly fond of Wagner's "Parsifal" and the works of Colombian composer Alberto Villalon, and he loved to play the haunting melodies for her. In Karl Tanzler's mind, he and Elena were a married couple, and he was enthralled to be her strong, sensitive lover.

Nine years had passed since her sister's death, and Florinda "Nana" Medina was troubled to hear the rumors about her sister's body growing louder. Shopkeepers whispered that Tanzler, now long unemployed, continued to purchase negligees, lingerie, women's jewelry, perfume, flowers, and cosmetics. She took her concerns to law enforcement but could not enlist their support. Finally, she decided to confront him at the graveyard. He held the only key to the vault with her sister's remains. She told him to open it, but he politely refused and asked her to come meet with him at his home instead. She agreed.

At Tanzler's home, he said little but guided her into his bedroom and, with a flourish, pulled back the curtains on the bed next to his. To Nana's horror, her sister seemed to stare back at her, though with lifeless, unblinking eyes. She was clad in a white bridal gown and wore a wedding band on her left ring finger. Nana recoiled in horror. For a few moments, she could not summon her tongue to work. The only parts of her sister that remained were her hair and bones, but Nana was racked by waves of nausea, horrified in one breath, incensed in the next. Finally, she spat out an ultimatum: In one week, her sister's remains must be returned to the vault in the mausoleum.

The week passed and Nana returned, this time with police. Karl Tanzler had dressed Elena in a blue silk kimono and posed her holding a rose. Tanzler was arrested and sent to jail. Elena's remains were sent back to Lopez Funeral Home, where they were put on public display. Nearly seven thousand people, many of them dragging their children along with them, attended the viewing. Media from all over the world sent correspondents to cover the too-weird-to-be-true tale of the grandfatherly man and his young, dead lover. The salacious details of the case that leaked out gave them plenty to write about.

Karl Tanzler, though his actions reviled some, was hardly looked upon as a pariah. Key West residents paid his bail and provided him with accommodations and board. An attorney stepped forward to represent him pro bono. People sent the eccentric old man money.

After Tanzler was ruled competent, the trial for grave-robbing turned out to be anticlimactic. Justice of the Peace Enrique Esquinaldo ruled that the statute of limitations had run out, and Tanzler was freed. He asked Esquinaldo if he could take Elena's remains with him, but the judge refused because Karl was not a relative of hers. The remains were turned over to Nana Medina.

Life after the trial was more difficult for Tanzler. During his confinement and while waiting for the trial, he was the center of attention in town and the regular beneficiary of the kindness of strangers. After the trial, interest waned. For a while, he gave twenty-five-cent tours of his home and the wingless airplane where he had kept Elena. But the media went on to other assignments, and the crowds dwindled.

The Hoyos family and the authorities realized that it would be difficult to give Elena Hoyos a final resting place that Karl

Tanzler or the curious would not again desecrate. Police Chief Benvenido Perez, cemetery sexton Otto Bethel, and Lopez Funeral Home mortician Ben Sawyer worked out a plan. Just as Tanzler had spirited Elena from her vault during the dead of night, they too executed their plan under the light of the moon. They stripped Elena's remains of the wax, wire, plaster, and other fasteners and placed the bones in a small wooden box, then buried the remains somewhere on the island. Bethel, Perez, and Sawyer swore they would carry the secret location to their own graves, and they did.

Feeling at the end of his wits, Karl Tanzler decided to move his belongings and his wingless airplane to be near his sister and his former wife, Doris, a nurse, who lived in Zephyrhills near Tampa. Dressed in a bow tie, fedora, and tennis shoes, Tanzler left Key West at 9 P.M. on April 14, 1941. His entourage included an eight-ton van and another truck to lug the crippled airplane. At 1:45 A.M., almost five hours later, an explosion rocked the city. Someone had placed two sticks of dynamite atop Elena's vault in the city cemetery and blew the mausoleum to rubble.

A few hundred miles north in Central Florida, in rural eastern Pasco County, the quiet city of Zephyrhills has few tourist attractions but lots of citrus trees. Zephyrhills is part of the citrus belt, and like its next-door neighboring community Crystal Springs, it is well known for its refreshing, clean-tasting drinking water. Zephyrhills bills itself as the "City of Pure Water."

Karl Tanzler settled in and worked quietly in Zephyrhills, preparing his memoirs for publication. He socialized little, and finally he seemed to fall off the radar screen entirely. Authorities became concerned and eventually decided to enter his home. There they found his decomposing corpse. He had been dead for up to five weeks. He was 75.

When they searched his home, they found a lifesize replica of Elena Hoyos, the woman whose beautiful face haunted him and remained in his every waking moment. There were also photo albums filled with pictures of her and a wax model of her head.

Not far from the center of town in Zephyrhills is Oakview Cemetery, the final resting place of noble heroes from six wars. It's also the final destination of the Tanzler family, a group certainly more bizarre than the Addams clan. Just at the fringe of shade between two of the spreading oaks that line the borders of the cemetery are the graves of Karl, Doris, and Crystal Tanzler. Karl's grave is marked only by a simple stone cross with peeling white paint. He was buried there on August 14, 1952.

Though she died in 1977, Doris Tanzler's grave, just to the left of her husband's, is still marked with a temporary grave marker. The grave of Crystal Tanzler, the younger of the couple's two daughters, lies at the feet of her father. Crystal, born in 1924, died of diphtheria at age 10. Her grave is the most ornate of the three, with an arched headstone decorated in terracotta cherubs painted white. The tablet beneath the arch carries a simple inscription:

Crystal Tanzler
Our darling

Back in Key West, the headstone from Elena's grave survived the blast and is on display in the East Martello Tower. On breezy nights, the locals say, you can sometimes catch a glimpse of Karl Tanzler, his shoulders stooped and his back hunched, shuffling slowly along Frances Street on the way to the cemetery. There is not much else to remind people of the tragic life and death of the raven-haired woman who died too young and the lovelorn old man who was obsessed with her.

The Haunted Lighthouse

Lighthouses are rich in ghostly legend and lore, from coast to coast in the United States as well as abroad. Screwpile lighthouses were perfectly suited for many Florida locations because of their unique construction, which secured the lighthouses deep into coral reefs with iron pilings. South Florida especially needed the screwpile lighthouses, because there are so many reefs lying just under the water's surface, waiting to trap unwary mariners.

But pity the desolation of the screwpile lighthouse keeper. Whereas a land-based lighthouse keeper could live with his family on the property, raise a garden, play with his children, and maybe even work in some time for fishing, the screwpile lighthouse keeper, held captive on what looks like a giant erector set on anabolic steroids, could enjoy only the last pastime, although some were able to bring their wives aboard. Each day the scene remained essentially the same: more water, more sky. Only the weather changed. At the Carysfort Lighthouse, almost every night's solitude was broken up by the noises of the night, the moans, shrieks, and screams compliments, some insist, of Captain Charles Johnson.

Carysfort Reef was named for HMS *Carysford,* a British frigate that ran aground on the reef in October 1770. Somehow, over the years, the "d" at the end of the name got changed to a "t." The first light placed on the reef was aboard a lightship, placed into service in 1824. Constantly blown onto the reef and damaged, that ship, the *Caesar,* was replaced by another, the *Florida.* In 1848, construction commenced on a 112-foot permanent beacon, using the iron screwpile design created by Alexander Mitchell in 1836. The Carysfort Reef Lighthouse was designed by Thomas Lannard and Harold Stanbury and was partially assembled in Philadelphia, then shipped to the site for installation.

Army Lieutenant George Gordon Meade, who went on to attain the rank of general and command the Union forces during the Battle of Gettysburg, supervised completion of the Carysfort Reef Lighthouse, the first of six screwpile lighthouses still lighting the way for mariners along the Florida coastline. Construction took four grueling years, and the lighthouse was placed into service on March 10, 1852.

Until 1960, keepers stayed in the two-story octagonal quarters and pulled six ten-hour shifts for two weeks, then received a free week ashore. Then the lighthouse was automated, and in 1970, solar panels were installed to harness the sun's power to operate the light.

Captain Charles Johnson was keeper for the *Florida* lightship and subsequently was named first keeper of the permanent beacon. Hearing what was said to be his ghost's ranting, raving, and wailing in the early evening was disconcerting to visitors to the lighthouse, but the sounds were good-naturedly accepted by the corps of keepers. Skeptics say the loud moans and groans were the result of the metal contracting as it cooled in the evening, but no one knows for sure, because no one's there to listen anymore. Today the lighthouse, located twelve miles northeast of Key Largo, is off-limits to visitors.

The area around the lighthouse is well liked by fishers, snorkelers, and scuba divers because the reef fish are plentiful, the underwater scenery is spectacular, and few divers venture that far off the coast.

The Demon Dolls

Robert Eugene Otto and his wife, Annette Parker Otto, reigned supreme as Key West's power couple during their day. Annette, better known as Anne, was a Bostonian by birth and one of America's best jazz pianists. She studied in Paris and had performed at the Rainbow Room in New York. Her husband was a Key West native, or "conch," and the youngest son of Dr. Thomas Otto, a prominent local physician. Robert Otto had studied painting in New York, Chicago, and Paris. Together the Ottos lived what seemed to be the good life in a beautiful home Robert Otto's father had owned and the family had occupied since 1898. Both were civic-minded citizens and worked diligently to improve Key West.

The Ottos were animal lovers too, devoted owners of Yorkies and a pet deer named Elfina. But life was not as perfect for the couple as it may have seemed from the outside. That was because of the influence of Robert, the demon doll.

A Haitian girl had given Robert Otto the doll when he was a young boy. It was practically as tall as he was. It wore sailor's whites and had a crude, simianlike face and dark, lifeless eyes as penetrating as a shark's. Otto was told the doll was very special because it had crystals sewn into its head.

Otto gave the doll his first name upon receiving it and never referred to himself as Robert again; from that moment on, he called himself Gene. When things went wrong, he was quick to blame the problems on Robert. And around Robert, things went wrong often.

Otto's relationship with Robert seemed unnatural enough when Otto was alive, but after his death in 1974, Robert began to make impressions on his own. Sometimes children would stop on the sidewalk across from the Ottos' Eaton Street home to wave at Robert in the turret. Robert, they said, waved back. Workmen who came into the house claimed to be unnerved by the doll, which, they said, changed positions as they worked. They'd complain of tools disappearing—yet the tools always seemed to return later.

Anne Otto lived until 1976. After her death, some say she stayed on at the Eaton Street home to watch over things. Robert, however, is no longer one of her concerns. Since 1994, he has been behind glass, locked in a case at the East Martello Museum. Those who keep tabs on him say that he's not getting into much mischief anymore, although he sometimes changes positions in the case. Psychics say the energy they once detected in him is flickering out.

As unsettling as Robert was, the doll that vanished from the Audubon House, just down Whitehead Street from Ernest Hemingway's island home, takes the prize for creepiness.

Made in England in the mid-1800s, this doll looked like a tiny zombie. Her face was as white as alabaster, with dark circles under the eyes. Her teeth were yellow, her expression vapid. And whenever people brought cameras around her, strange things happened. Rolls of film popped out of the cameras, and pictures of her had portions blacked out or failed to develop. Guests to the home say the doll watched them in the room.

Strange things happened in the upstairs areas of the house too. Lights were turned off and on by unseen hands. Rooms developed cold spots, and items rearranged themselves.

One day the doll disappeared. It hasn't been seen since, and Audubon House operates normally again.

The Artist House, home of Gene and Anne Otto, at 534 Eaton Street in Key West, today is a bed-and-breakfast. The Audubon House and Tropical Gardens, at 250 Whitehead Street, is a museum.

The Space Coast and the Heartland

FLORIDA'S MIDSECTION IS FILLED WITH UNUSUAL AND SOMETIMES confounding places, odd happenings, and some very interesting people, including Florida's indigenous citizens, spiritualists who came to find a quiet environment where they could communicate with the departed, and folks with their heads in the clouds. The Space Coast, where man's dreams for the future take wing, is an area thought to have a rather incredibly haunted past. To its west, the Heartland region has blossomed from orange groves, farms, grasslands, and pine forests into a tourist mecca like none other.

Few places so nobly represent man's aspirations for the future as the Space Coast, and the Heartland of Central Florida is a world-class destination for fun. But in the dark, a different side emerges.

Ashley's Ghosts

Ashley's Café and Lounge, at 1609 South U.S. Highway 1 in Rockledge, does not merely acknowledge its haunted reputation, it celebrates it. Etched on the glass in the front door is the image of a ghost dressed in top hat and tails. Framed magazine and newspaper articles about the eerie phenomena there are in evidence throughout the restaurant.

Housed in a Tudor-style building between U.S. 1 and the railroad tracks, Ashley's is a pleasant place—the kind of spot you'd go to enjoy a weekend football game on big-screen TV with friends while munching on sandwiches or Buffalo chicken wings and quaffing rounds of frosty, frothy beverages. Laughter and camaraderie are abundant.

But Ashley's, which has been known by many names over its long history, also has a dark side. Step into the women's restroom, and the window there may slam shut for no reason. When the stall door opens, an apparition of a woman in 1920s-style clothing may breeze by you.

Inside the restaurant, a wide variety of poltergeist activity has been reported, but the most interesting action seems to take place in the dark, quiet hours after the staff has cleaned up and gone home. Once a photographer stayed late to get a picture of the empty main dining room. When he developed the photo, he found an unmistakable human image in the midst of the room, yet he was positive no one was there when he took the picture. A scent-free, smokelike stream has been known to waft through the building on occasion as well.

Much of the ghostly behavior has been attributed to Ethel Allen, said to have been murdered at age eighteen in a storeroom at Ashley's in 1934. Her remains were found alongside the Indian River in Eau Gallie. She is buried at Georgiana Graveyard

in Merritt Island. A telltale mark—the tattoo of a flower—was cut from her leg before her body was dumped.

Spiritualism at Cassadaga

Just outside the municipal limits of the city of Lake Helen in far western Volusia County sits Cassadaga, or more formally, the Southern Cassadaga Spiritualist Camp Meeting Association, a fifty-seven-acre parcel where spirits roam freely. Cassadaga is the oldest active religious community in the United States.

To be one of the hundred or so residents of Cassadaga, one must be a member of the association. Mediums on the grounds must be registered with the association and abide by its standards of practice. Residents own the fifty-five homes in the community, but the land on which those homes are built is owned by the association.

Cassadaga got its start in 1875, when George P. Colby, a New York medium, guided by instructions he received during a séance, traveled to Florida's wilderness Heartland to select a site for settlement. Colby was suffering from tuberculosis when he arrived in Central Florida, and he found that the water from a spring on his homestead made his symptoms better, eventually allowing him to recover and lead a full life.

Colby formally created Cassadaga in 1894, and the next year he deeded more than thirty-five acres of his seventy-four-acre homestead to the association. Marion Skidmore and Emma Huff, two mediums from the Lily Dale Assembly in New York, joined Colby there, and the fledgling community began to grow slowly. An important tenet for the camp association was to establish an educational center where Spiritualism could be taught.

Today Cassadaga, at County Road 4139 at Stevens Street near I-4, appears to be a quaint, sleepy southern town, with vernacular homes lining the roadways. It continues to move along at its own pace, welcoming believers, questioners, and skeptics; teaching about Spirituality; and offering its services to those who seek help and enlightenment. Persons who wish to heighten their spiritual awareness flock there so that they can get better in touch with themselves or loved ones on the other side. Mediums and spiritual healers are available for readings and spiritual healing during the day. At night, séances and circles are offered to contact and communicate with the departed. Ghost hunters and paranormal researchers have found the community rich for exploration as well.

Saturdays are especially good days for visitors, with "Encounter the Spirit" walking tours in the afternoon and orb photography classes offered in the evening.

The Playful Little Ghost

The handsome Spanish-style building at 19 New Haven Avenue in Melbourne was originally the home of William Preston Sloan and his family. Sloan was called "Doc" for the popular Sloan's Liniment sold during the era. William Sloan was the purveyor of powerful potions too, smuggling alcohol to thirsty Central Floridians during Prohibition. His wife, Mattie Mae Brannen, designed the prosperous family's showcase home on what was then the far western reaches of Melbourne. George Fowler constructed the home in early 1926, and Sloan ran his business from the family showplace.

On March 31 of that year, the Sloans welcomed about a hundred of the city's power elite for housewarming festivities. Two months after the happy occasion, the family suffered tragedy when two-year-old daughter Cora Elizabeth was fatally burned in a fire believed to have been caused by her playing with matches.

The family's misfortunes continued after the little girl's death. Sloan was arrested, tried, and served a short prison term in an Atlanta penitentiary for bootlegging. Upon his return, the family pulled up stakes and moved to Fort Pierce, but little Cora's spirit apparently stayed behind. She was playful and mischievous, fiddling with the lights, moving things around, and generally playing harmless little pranks. Some guests heard footsteps in the locked upstairs sections, and others reported faint sounds.

The Sloan home served as a residence facility for Navy personnel and their families, a clinic, private hospital, and convalescent center. It later was fitted out as a Mexican-Spanish restaurant called Miguel's Posada del Rey. After a fire, the building was razed, and in 2003, a CVS Pharmacy was built on the property. Pharmacy personnel report no sightings of little Cora today.

Murray's Mischievous Poltergeist

Murray's Coffee to a Tea, a pleasant British-style restaurant and tearoom in Indiatlantic constructed from an early 1920s-era vernacular home, is but a memory now. The building was razed to make way for condominiums. During its time, Murray's was known as much for the mischievous poltergeist that played tricks on the staff as it was for its famed chunky chicken salad sandwiches.

No one was ever quite sure who the poltergeist was. There was no record of death or violence in the building when it was used as a house or a restaurant. Some said it was the spirit of a little girl; others believed it was an older man. Whoever it was, it had a puckish sense of humor, sliding glasses off shelves and counters, knocking utensils around, and hiding the staff's personal items, such as pens and eyeglasses.

By night, psychics used Murray's for readings, as they found the atmosphere conducive to communicating with the other side.

The Suncoast

FLORIDA'S SUNCOAST EXTENDS ROUGHLY FROM TARPON SPRINGS, AT the northern end of Pinellas County, south to Chokoloskee Island, the southernmost point in Collier County and the western gateway to the Everglades. Within that territory lie Tampa Bay and the cities of Tampa, St. Petersburg, Clearwater, Fort Myers, and more.

The warm, pleasant waters of the Gulf of Mexico long have attracted tourists and retirees alike, but years ago, they also attracted pirates such as the infamous Jose Gaspar, better known as Gasparilla. The last of the buccaneers, Gasparilla plied the waters of the Gulf until he was a very old man. The bay area as well as the offshore islands provided safe harbor for him and others hiding from something . . . or someone. It should not be surprising, then, that some of the stories of ghosts and haunts from this region take place in this setting.

The Ghost Who Won't Check Out

In the late 1890s, Thomas Rowe went to Europe to attend school. It was there that he met Lucinda, the love of his life. The two would often meet in a nearby courtyard and stroll hand in hand around a fountain. That is, until her parents discovered the romance and forbade the couple to see each other. Rowe left Europe heartbroken but promised to return for his beloved.

In 1925, Rowe began building her a palace in which to live. He oversaw construction during the day and wrote loving letters to Lucinda by night. Slowly, the pink walls of the Don CeSar Hotel began to take shape on St. Petersburg Beach. Ever thoughtful, Rowe also included a replica of the courtyard and fountain where he and Lucinda used to meet.

When it opened in 1928, the hotel, better known as "the Don," quickly became the hot spot for high society, both debutantes and despots, the famous and the infamous. Among its guests were F. Scott Fitzgerald, Clarence Darrow, Lou Gehrig, and Al Capone. But sadly, Lucinda wasn't among them. Though the palace was lovingly constructed for her, she never spent even one night under its roof. She died before making the trip there. After word of her death reached him, Rowe received a package from overseas. It was all the letters he had written—still unopened.

Shattered, Rowe lived in the Don until his death. When he died without a will, his long-estranged wife became the heir, and the resort soon fell into disrepair.

After the onset of World War II, the U.S. Army purchased the property and turned it into a convalescent home for soldiers. After the war, it became a Veterans Administration regional office, until the government could no longer afford necessary repairs on the once stately resort.

Abandoned from 1967 to 1973, the pink palace fell further into disrepair, and vandals covered its walls with graffiti. A series of renovations from 1973 to 1989 transformed the Spanish interiors to a more modern, Continental look. Another multimillion-dollar renovation in 1994 and yet another just recently have combined to make this resort at 3400 Gulf Boulevard a beautiful getaway for travelers from around the world—though it's still apparently home to one very settled-in ghost.

Dressed in a dark suit and wearing a Panama hat, Rowe is sometimes seen and heard overseeing his property, apparently unwilling to check out of the castle he built for his unrequited love. There have been so many noise complaints from guests that several years ago, management built a special room between floors just for Rowe and asked him to please stay put, because he was upsetting the paying guests.

The hotel has hosted haunted tours, regaling guests with Rowe's exploits throughout the years. Maintenance workers have reported knocks on doors when no living person could have made them. And although the fountain was removed in one of the many renovations of the resort, employees of the Don still recall seeing a couple suddenly appear walking hand in hand in the hotel . . . then disappearing.

Jack Kerouac's Bookstore Haunt

Housed in a building that dates to the 1920s, Haslam's Book Store, at 2025 Central Avenue in St. Petersburg, contains more than three hundred thousand new and used books and has been in the same family since 1933. Begun as a small newspaper and magazine stand by avid readers John and Mary Haslam, the store is now the largest independent bookstore in Florida and a mecca for bibliophiles. It was named one of the top twenty-five independent bookstores in the United States by bookmarket.com. Today it is operated by the third generation of Haslams, Suzanne Haslam Hinst and husband Ray Hinst Jr., who have run the store since 1973 and have seen, felt, and heard it all about their store.

Jack Kerouac, a poster boy of the Beat Generation, was no stranger around bookstores. In San Francisco, the famed City Lights was his hangout, along with luminary friends Allen Ginsberg, Lawrence Ferlinghetti, and others. After years spent shuttling between points on the compass, Kerouac spent his last years in St. Petersburg, by duty, not choice. The fire in his belly was not fully extinguished, though it had been suppressed. He felt forced to stay in St. Petersburg to care for his ill mother and mollify his demanding wife. While in Florida, alcohol allowed him to make his miserable existence more palatable.

Trips to Haslam's helped too. He'd lurch hungover into the store to rearrange his and his buddies' books to give them better play on the shelves. Apparently he continues to do so today, even though he's been dead since 1969.

Ray Hinst was working late one night restocking the shelves when a book dropped onto the store's tile floor, shattering the silence. The incident unnerved him, since books in that section of the store were shelved upright, spines outward, snuggled as tight as ticks to one another. Hinst walked to where the book lay. It was Kerouac's autobiographical novel, *On the Road*, lying faceup.

Occasionally people come into the store to ask if it is really haunted by the author's ghost. Some are just idle curiosity seekers, others are fans of Kerouac, and still others are ghost hunters wanting to bump into the disembodied poet themselves.

Haslam's remains popular not only among tourists, bibliophiles and its loyal customers, but also among psychics, paranormal investigators and even skeptics. Some perhaps come to find a spiritual connection to the wild-eyed, unkempt, unpredictable Kerouac, but others visit in an attempt to find more rational explanations for what has been observed there. One ghost-hunting group concluded the store was home to a corps of benevolent spirits: a studious couple, a milquetoast man, a rambunctious little boy, a morose girl, and others.

The alcohol that Kerouac drank far too much of also served as a corrosive. On an October morning in 1969, the lining of the stomach of the spokesman of the Beat Generation gave way, and he began throwing up blood. It didn't stop. He died at 47 on October 21 in St. Anthony's Hospital.

His visits to Haslam's during his mortal years were sometimes loud, vulgar, and unpleasant, but Kerouac is a welcome visitor there, now that he is dead. The store shows him respect, shelving his books in prime, eye-level spots. And with that, Jack Kerouac's visits to the store have become quieter and less frequent.

The Other Koresh

On a quiet summer weekday, the stillness on the grounds at the Koreshan State Historic Site is eerie, especially as you realize that the hustle and bustle of the Tamiami Trail, U.S. 41, is just on the other side of the clumps of bamboo, yards away from the eastern edge of the property. It was on this quiet, lovely 305-acre plot of land that Cyrus Reed Teed and his followers arrived in 1894 hoping to create New Jerusalem, a perfect, thirty-six-mile-square self-sustaining religious community. Teed envisioned that the quiet settlement would grow to become one of the great and enlightened cities of history, home to as many as ten million devotees.

Born in New York in 1839, a distant cousin of Joseph Smith, founder of the Church of Jesus Christ of Latter-Day Saints, Teed was a handsome, charismatic young man who bore an uncanny likeness to actor Anthony Hopkins. He grappled with his career choices and eventually chose medicine over religion after serving a stint in the Union Army Medical Corps. After earning his medical degree from the New York Eclectic School of Medicine in New York City, he established a successful practice near Syracuse, but he grew disillusioned with medicine and turned to the study of alchemy. It was in northern New York that Teed experienced his "divine illumination" in 1869, when he believed that the secrets of spirituality were revealed to him. Teed took on the name Koresh, the translation of his first name into Hebrew. He professed that his illumination made him immortal and compelled him to lead people who sought enlightenment to create the perfect utopian community.

He moved to Chicago, where he tried to start a commune in 1888, but he was rebuffed by nonbelievers in the local community. A compelling and energetic speaker, Teed persevered, found followers quickly, and housed them in a decaying mansion. Koreshan Unity, as the movement was called, offered a life of prayer, education, work, and play with like-minded people in a wholesome atmosphere without crime or drugs. All social, economic, and spiritual needs were met. To top it all off, he promised reincarnation, too.

The settlement was no monastery. Education, cultural activities, and even other forms of entertainment were provided. The inner circle of worshipers, called the Religious Order, went a step further, giving up their worldly possessions and living a life of celibacy. Teed was married to Fidelia Rowe, who bore a son, Douglas Arthur Teed. Douglas Teed became an artist, and many of his paintings hang today in the Art Hall on the Home Grounds.

Teed and the Koreshans moved to Estero from their Chicago headquarters in 1894 on the invitation of Gustave Damkohler. They found their faith severely tested in steamy, searing, mosquito-infested Florida, yet they persevered. They set about carving their New Jerusalem out of the scrub and mangroves, planting mangoes and other fruit trees, and creating commercial and light industries on the Home Grounds that would generate revenue for the community. These included an apiary, bakery, boat-building shop, concrete company, general store, large and small machine shops, publishing house, sawmill, rustic tea garden, and much later, a trailer park.

They moved goods in and out on the Estero River, which flowed along the north edge of their settlement. The Tamiami Trail was constructed in the early 1920s and further exposed them to the outside world. All the while, they purchased land, eventually amassing nearly eight thousand acres.

The Koreshans, though they stayed and worked together on the settlement property, were something of an oddity to the locals, but they worked hard to blend in when they needed to. When they traveled or were out in public, they were very aware of making their dress modest yet contemporary. The lessons Teed learned over his first failed commune were not lost on him, but the surrounding community didn't totally accept the Koreshans, particularly as they began participating in local politics.

Among the tenets of Koreshanity were the absolute biunity of men and women, a rare concept during that time. The concept of equality, Teed said, did not exist, but the principle of equity for men and women alike was a natural law. Teed, as Koreshanity's founder, was the central figure in the community, but the group's first president, Annie Ordway (later known as Victoria Gratia) was a woman, and the Planetary Chamber, ruling council of the community, was composed of seven women who lived together in the relatively opulent Planetary Court building.

Koreshans believed that heaven and hell were conditions of the mind, rather than the natural or spiritual world, and that the Bible is an excellent expression of the Divine Creator but required the intervention of prophets throughout the ages to make it completely relevant to believers. Koreshanity did not seek to rebuke Christianity or Judaism, merely to redefine and refine it and allow its practitioners to experience it in a purer setting. A sign in the Art Hall reinforces the belief: "Koreshanity defends the faith of the Jews in the Old Testament and of the Christians in both Old and New Testaments."

The most enduring and interesting concept of Koreshanity is its theory of cosmogony, the belief that the universe is not a vast expanse, but a hollow globe that holds within it all forms of life on its concave inner surface. To show that this theory was true and make the sect more attractive to converts, Teed and his followers set about attempting to prove it through the Koreshanity Premise: "A straight line extended at right angles to a perpendicular over land or water will meet the water or surface of the earth at a distance proportionate to the height of the perpendicular."

Early attempts in Chicago had been unsuccessful, but on the Naples beach, Teed's devotees erected a "geodesic rectilineator" of wood and steel to prove the Koreshanity Premise correct. Locals watched the Koreshans build and operate the rectilineator. The Koreshans announced that their experiments had proved the premise correct, and in 1899, they released a guide explaining the experiments, the significance of the results, and the confirmation of the theory of cosmogony.

But the hoped-for flood of new converts was more of a trickle, and local tensions with the surrounding community were growing. In October 1906, after a Koreshan candidate for public office was accosted by one of the locals, Teed met with the candidate, a town marshal, and the assailant. During their review of the incident, the assailant punched Teed several times in the head and face. Witnesses said the marshal joined in the attack. Teed never fully recovered, suffering from an excruciating, debilitating condition that grew worse over the months that followed. Teed eventually withdrew from his role as founder of the sect and moved to a cottage on Estero Island in the hope that rest and solitude could help him recover, but instead, his condition deteriorated, and he died on December 22, 1908.

Confident of his eventual reincarnation, his followers lovingly buried him in a concrete mausoleum next to the cottage where he spent his last days. The simple headstone read, "Cyrus, Shepherd, Stone of Israel." An October 1921 hurricane washed away the cottage and the huge, heavy mausoleum. Only the headstone was recovered.

Without Teed's robust personality leading the group, and with his promise of his reincarnation unfulfilled, the community foundered. Several groups splintered off, but all eventually failed. The last Koreshan was Hedwig Michel, a native of Germany who joined the sect in 1941, when it was severely in decline. Under her guidance, a building was completed in 1979 across the Tamiami Trail from the settlement to be used as an archive and repository of Koreshan memorabilia. She also was a force behind the donation in 1961 of 110 acres to the state for the Koreshan State Historic Site, located at the northwest corner of U.S. 41 (Tamiami Trail) at Corkscrew Road. Michel died in 1982 and was buried on the Home Ground, the only Koreshan buried there. Ironically, many Koreshans were interred in a burial ground hidden behind a ring of pine trees in what is now Pelican Sound, a posh golf course community.

The Koreshan Unity Settlement Historic District was listed on the National Register of Historic Places in 1976. College of Life Foundation, established in 1987 as the Koreshan Unity Alliance, Inc., is a nonprofit organization that continues the work of Koreshan Unity and acts as conservators of the church and community artifacts and documents.

Each year on the weekend nearest the full moons in January and February, several dozen volunteers portray Teed and his followers in the annual Koreshan Ghost Walks, which depict life at the Home Ground. The sound of dozens of pairs of feet crunching along the eerie crushed-shell paths combine with shadows and lots of Spanish moss to provide a spooky but enlightening experience. Folks sometimes say they hear disembodied footsteps during the walks, and they wonder if it is Teed. After all, he promised everyone he was coming back.

Mrs. Reeser's Bizarre Demise

For years, tenants in the eggshell-colored apartment building have reported things that go bump in the night. They have heard strange sounds that they absolutely could not attribute to a logical cause. Most believe the noises, bumps, and brouhaha came from its longtime ghostly inhabitant, Mary Reeser, who met her demise in the corner apartment in the middle of the last century.

Early on July 2, 1951, Mary Hardy Reeser, a plump, likable chain smoker, sat alone in her easy chair in St. Petersburg's Allamanda Apartments. Little did she know her nodding off in her studio apartment would cause a national commotion. When her son left her the previous evening, she had popped a sleeping pill and planned to watch TV to calm her nerves. She was happy and excited because she had learned her plans for a trip to Pennsylvania were confirmed, and as a result, her nerves were still a little raw from a day of waiting. That's why she took the sedative.

Early the next morning, the landlady at the apartments caught a whiff of smoke but couldn't pinpoint its origin. She thought little of it. Later, a telegraph arrived bearing confirmation of Mrs. Reeser's travel plans, and the landlady dispatched the handyman to deliver it. He reached for the door of the apartment and found it blistering hot. The police and fire departments were summoned.

When firefighters knocked down her door at 8 A.M., they were surprised by the scene in the ashes before them. All that remained of Reeser was her slippered left foot and ankle. Her skull had shrunk to the size of an orange. There were almost no traces of the black acetate nightgown and robe she had been wearing, but parts of the room had been unaffected by the fire. The chair in which she had been sitting was burned away, leaving just the springs. An end table near the chair was partially consumed. The carpet was burned in the area where the chair had been.

The FBI was summoned for a more meticulous investigation, but there was a paucity of evidence. The electrical system was sound. Lab results showed no traces of chemicals to ignite, accelerate or sustain a fire hot enough to incinerate Reeser. Many jumped to the conclusion that spontaneous human combustion was the cause of her death.

The story spread like wildfire. It was reported widely across the country in newspapers and on the radio. People came from all over to see where this phenomenon had taken place. Folks fretted that it could happen to them. And soon the ghost stories began to circulate.

The police and fire departments chose to believe that Reeser's tragic death had come as a result of being struck by a bolt of lightning. Some postulated that an electrical fire was the cause. The partial remains of a cigarette lighter were found at the scene. Could the explanation be as simple as Reeser falling into a drug-induced sleep while smoking? She was a heavy woman, and a cigarette would have had time to smolder in the chair stuffing. Her body fat could have fueled the fire yet allowed it to remain contained. Her skull would have shrunken as a result of the intense heat of the fire and its accelerant.

Or perhaps she really did spontaneously combust and is doomed to haunt the apartments at 1200 Cherry Street NE, making things go bump in the night. For years, friends and family said they sensed her presence at the apartment and often caught a whiff of the distinctive perfume she always wore. The FBI never did determine exactly what happened, and her death remains officially unsolved.

Phantoms at the Vinoy

Built in just ten months in 1925, the Renaissance Vinoy Resort and Golf Club opened its doors in December and was one of the finest examples of Mediterranean Revival architecture in Florida. Today it is the showplace of St. Petersburg's waterfront, the only luxury resort on Florida's West Coast with a private marina, eighteen-hole golf course, and twelve-court tennis complex. The meticulously restored resort at 501 Fifth Avenue NE has earned a National Register of Historic Places designation.

The well-appointed luxury hotel that once welcomed U.S. Presidents Herbert Hoover and Calvin Coolidge and movie stars Jimmy Stewart and Marilyn Monroe as guests is now the official home to the Tampa Bay Rays' visiting teams. The Vinoy also houses an unofficial apparition or two. And a few current celebrities can attest to their presence.

Former Cincinnati Reds pitcher Scott Williamson said that during his stay at the Vinoy, he was visited by a ghost. After feeling as though someone were pushing down on him as he slept, Williamson awakened to find a man standing at the end of his bed, watching over him. Williamson tried to focus more clearly and saw that the man's clothing and hairstyle were those popular in an earlier time. Several major-league heavy hitters who have stayed in the resort have encountered the same nocturnal visitor who wears the same style clothes and same haircut. He just stands at the player's bedside, then vanishes. Other players have reported other odd incidents: faucets turning on and off by themselves, toilets flushing several times in a row, doors opening that had been bolted closed.

Others who don't trot around the baseball diamond for a living claim to have seen a different apparition in the Vinoy. Some say they can see the vaporous Lady in White in the fifth-floor corridor. They say she is the ghost of a woman allegedly pushed down the stairs to her death. Others claim that the Lady in White is the victim's maid, who witnessed the attack but mysteriously disappeared before she could testify.

The Skunk Ape

The Skunk Ape, southwestern Florida's version of Bigfoot or Sasquatch, was first observed by a pair of hunters in 1957. He's been seen sporadically since then by a handful of folks, most of them locals involved in the tourist trade or tourists on airboat or swamp buggy tours of the Big Cypress Swamp. After you've seen your first dozen alligators, they all start looking the same, and after you've seen one cypress knee, you've seen them all. Searching for the simian of the swamp is far more exciting than the panorama of thousands of soggy acres of sawgrass.

After falling into a lull, Skunk Ape mania was resuscitated with a Collier County resident's 1997 picture of the Skunk Ape in a pine thicket. Then a British tourist snapped a shot, and another picture taken a year later on the grasslands shows the creature more clearly. The picture suggests that he is seven to eight feet tall, with a little flab as part of his three hundred or so pounds. He also appears to be covered with reddish brown fur. His face is largely flat and covered with hair too.

What the pictures don't show is the stench. Those who claim to have seen the Skunk Ape say the particular aroma that emanates from him is a malodorous marriage of aged sewage, animal feces, rotten eggs, and overripe Limburger cheese.

He's said to rip women's underwear off clotheslines and enjoy eating dried lima beans, but these seem to be the only interests he has in getting close to his *Homo sapiens* cousins.

Though most of the Skunk Ape sightings have been from around Ochopee to the Everglades City area, he apparently is peripatetic, because he also has been sighted throughout Central Florida around the Myakka River as well as Melbourne and as far north as Jacksonville. Or there may be another explanation: Recent reports indicate there may be multiple Skunk Apes, but all seem to want to stay out of the public's eye.

The Shadowy Specter on the Sunshine Skyway Bridge

The morning of May 9, 1980, was the kind most folks dread going to work in. The skies were gray, and patches of fog dotted the Tampa Bay area. Showers spattered water on weary motorists.

On the long Sunshine Skyway Bridge, motorists poked through the fog. The bridge had first been constructed as a four-mile ribbon connecting Pinellas and Manatee Counties, bypassing Hillsborough County. The original bridge was built for $22 million and opened on September 6, 1954. As the area grew, it became obvious the bridge was inadequate. In 1971, a second span was opened. It cost $25 million and was used for southbound traffic. The original bridge was adapted for northbound travel, giving the bridge side-by-side spans.

The big bridge was a boon for traffic but also attracted another element of Tampa Bay society—the depressed. The bridge seemed to draw those who contemplated or attempted suicide like a magnet, and as a result, it perhaps even had its own ghost. The shadowy image of a slender young woman with long hair, believed to be a hitchhiker who crawled over the railing and plunged to her death, was sometimes reported walking along the side of the bridge.

On that fateful morning in May 1980, harbor pilot John Lerro had boarded the 608-foot *Summit Venture* in the Gulf of Mexico about 6:25 A.M. with a trainee pilot, taking over control of the ship from Captain Hsuing Chu Lui. The big, tan vessel was riding high in the water as it headed toward the Port of Tampa to take on a load of phosphate bound for Asia.

As Lerro guided the vessel toward a dogleg in the ship channel, weather conditions in the bay deteriorated quickly. A squall blew in as the ship inched forward, and *Summit Venture*, hard to control because it was riding so high in the water, rammed into one of the pilings for the southbound lanes of the bridge, knocking 1,200 feet of the bridge into Tampa Bay. A bus, pickup truck, and six cars fell 150 feet, sending thirty-five victims to their death. One person survived. Just after 7:38 A.M., a radio transmission from Lerro crackled in the St. Petersburg Coast Guard office: "The Skyway Bridge is down . . . It's a mayday situation!"

Two days after the tragedy, the old 1954 span was converted back into a two-way thoroughfare, and traffic began crossing the bay again. Not long after the wreckage was cleared, planning began for a new Sunshine Skyway Bridge. The apparition of the depressed young woman was no longer reported.

The dramatic 5.5-mile, $244 million Bob Graham Sunshine Skyway Bridge opened on April 30, 1987, serving as I-275 and U.S. 19 from St. Petersburg to Terra Ceia. Among the amenities on the new bridge were crisis phones for those considering suicide and twenty-four-hour patrols who kept a wary eye for the forlorn and depressed. Parts of the old bridge remain and are used as fishing piers. The main span of the old 1954 bridge was demolished in 1993, and sometime thereafter, reports began again about the shadowy figure of a lean young woman with blond hair, seen walking along the side of the bridge and then simply vanishing.

The Treasure Coast

FLORIDA'S TREASURE COAST IS MADE UP OF THREE COASTAL COUNTIES: Indian River County at the northernmost point, then southward through St. Lucie County and on to Martin County at its southern end. Okeechobee County is considered by many to be a part of the Treasure Coast as well, but the only body of water it touches is Lake Okeechobee.

Not surprisingly, many of the stories from the Treasure Coast have a connection to the water or take place on or near it. The Treasure Coast's name comes from the many shipwrecks that took place there or just offshore, and those who searched for treasure or tried to steal it were in abundance in the days of yore.

The area also served as home to a different kind of treasure hunters—the Ashley Gang, a group of ruthless bank robbers and thieves who made the Treasure Coast their own personal treasure chest starting in 1911. The members of the Ashley Gang were surprised by a roadblock at a bridge at the Sebastian inlet, in northern Indian River County, and died in a gun battle with police officers on November 1, 1924.

Avenue A Apparitions

Nowadays, the offices at 217, 219, and 221 Avenue A, located on a tiny alcove along the quiet street in downtown Fort Pierce, hum with the sounds of everyday commerce, but that was not always the case. Years ago, when all the fuss started, the tiny storefronts served as a wig store and beauty shop. Employees in those and adjacent shops were troubled by wails and other sounds that reverberated through the building. They sent in plumbers, electricians, contractors, and other professionals to determine the cause of the noises but got no answers. Eventually they became so unnerved by the shrieks, wails, moans, and other sounds that they asked the building owner to try psychic means to end the disturbing sounds. They had failed at all other approaches.

The owner set up a session with a local psychic to confront the source of the noise and attempt to mollify it. About a dozen people participated in the session, and although no one saw anything, all smelled an undeniable yet indescribable scent at about the same time. Within seconds, most of the participants reported sensing the presence of a woman from the turn of the century, who communicated to them that she and her family had lived at the site, which was part of a rooming house then. The women's husband and son had gone off on a fishing trip and never returned. She had spent decades tearfully awaiting their return.

Any good psychotherapist knows that letting a troubled person speak freely to unburden herself has great therapeutic value, and apparently the same rings true in the spirit world. Since the session, calm has returned to the block, and the only noises that rumble through the buildings on Avenue A are caused by the trains at the end of the street.

Cresthaven's Ghosts

William T. Jones completed construction on Cresthaven, his three-story home, in 1909. He financed its construction with a $6,000 settlement from a disability suit against the railroad where he had worked as an engineer. The stately pillared edifice stood on the highest point in town and looked over Fort Pierce and the Indian River. The home boasted five bedrooms and two baths. Many of the building supplies were brought by railroad from Georgia, including bricks made of rich, red clay. Much of the interior woodwork was tough, durable Dade County pine. Jones's building supplies were hauled to the site via railroad. Southeastern Florida's prime developer, Henry Flagler, was a personal friend and saw to it.

Seemingly content to live in his beautiful home and manage his citrus groves in nearby Indian River County, Jones accepted the invitation to become sheriff in May 1915 after a simmering feud between U.S. Marshal D. J. Disney and Sheriff Dan Carlton erupted in a shootout on Pine Street in downtown Fort Pierce. Disney lost his right eye in the altercation and suffered a broken leg, but Carlton died. Governor Park Trammell appointed Jones, a well-respected man with a likable personality, to fill Carlton's post. Jones was reelected twice, but he resigned in 1920 in a salary dispute. He later lost Cresthaven during the Great Depression.

The home then served for a while as a boardinghouse and as a bed-and-breakfast inn. Some say that's when the Perkins family dropped by for a visit. Mr. Perkins checked in along with his wife, Aleacon, and their son Timmy. One morning, father and son went on a fishing trip, a popular activity in what many claim is the best sportfishing area in the nation. But Timmy and his father became lost in a storm at sea. The father's lifeless body washed ashore, but the son's never did. Some say it's Aleacon Perkins who silently roams the building at night, occasionally glancing out the third-floor window, waiting vigilantly for her beloved little boy to return.

At least Aleacon Perkins keeps quiet, or relatively so. Other noises in the building make it an unsettling place to be, especially during night, and most especially on those nights when the wind coming off the ocean kicks up, causing whistling and moaning sounds in addition to the bumping and thumping in the building and the screams, wails, and howls. Those working in the building at night say they've felt cold spots in some places, tiny blasts of heat in others. Others have reported they felt as though they'd been pushed or shoved by unseen hands.

The McCarty family, who owned and lived in the house across Boston Avenue, purchased Cresthaven in 1949 for $13,500 for use as an office building. A hero in World War II, Daniel T. McCarty Jr. served in the 1937 and 1939 sessions of the Florida legislature and was elected governor in 1952, but his term of office was short and tragic. He suffered a heart attack on February 25, 1953, and died seven months to the day later.

During the 1970s, the building's future seemed unclear and at times threatened, but in 1984, it was purchased for $195,000, a far cry from what the McCarty family had paid thirty-five years earlier. Cresthaven was named to the National Register of Historic Places in April 1985. Renovated in 1984–85, it is now better known as the Boston House. It is at 239 Indian River Drive and serves as a law office.

The Spirit of Trapper Nelson

The 11,500-acre Jonathan Dickinson State Park is at 16450 SE Federal Highway, at the south end of Martin County, a stone's throw from the Palm Beach County line. Visitors can take a tour boat ride through the park along the Loxahatchee River, named a National Wild and Scenic River in 1985. At the end of the trip is a visit to the home of Trapper Nelson, who arrived there in the

1930s and made his living as a trapper, selling pelts for coats for the famous and wealthy who lived in Palm Beach and beyond. He also sold fruit that grew wild on the property and trapped snakes and other small animals and sold them as pets.

Born Victor Nostokovich in Trenton, New Jersey, Nelson was a handsome, strapping man standing six feet, four inches and weighing 240 pounds. His path to advancement was limited by little education, but after moving to Florida in the 1930s, he thrived in the wilds and served as a steward of the Loxahatchee River.

Nelson committed suicide in 1968, although some say he was the victim of a very cleverly concocted murder plot. His spirit is said to have a strong presence at his home camp and has been experienced by both park personnel and visitors.

It is likely that Nelson might have decided not to go quietly into the afterlife because of the visitors who came at night to pluck the berries from the saw palmettos and sell them for a handsome profit. The abundant berries have wide medicinal value, especially as a urinary medication to ease the discomfort of benign prostatic hyperplasia. But the illegal harvest of the berries denied the park animals an important food source.

During World War II, the land the park occupies served as Camp Murphy, headquarters of the Southern Signal Corps School. The dense scrub that grows there was ideal in helping keep the camp clandestine. Most of the locals were unaware the camp was in their midst. Two Army buildings from Camp Murphy still exist on the site. One is now the park headquarters building. The site was opened to the public as a park in 1950 and is a favorite among outdoor-activity enthusiasts.

The Elliott Museum's Phantom Caretaker

The Elliott Museum, at 825 NE Ocean Boulevard on Hutchinson Island, was founded by seasonal Stuart resident Harmon P. Elliott in memory of his father, Sterling, an inventor with a particular interest in the automotive industry. Together the Elliotts were awarded more than 220 patents.

Although the rambling Elliott Museum has an impressive collection of motor-driven vehicles, it is more a tribute to American creativity and ingenuity. It has a little something for everyone, including a pearl-handled revolver once owned by a member of the infamous Ashley Gang, which terrorized South Florida in the 1920s and early 1930s.

After the tourists go home at night, the Elliott, as it is affectionately known, takes on a different complexion. The rooms develop cold spots, and drafts waft through the building. Doors open and close on their own, and lights sometimes turn themselves off and on. The carpeted floors creak, and disembodied footsteps pad around. Staff members don't particularly like to stay in the building alone at night.

Sterling Elliott died in 1922, but it is Harmon, who died in 1969, who is believed to be the source of the noises and other phenomena. He built the museum in 1960 and donated many of his and his father's inventions to it, so it seems likely he's simply watching out for a place that's very special to him.

The Happy Spirits of Gilbert's Bar House of Refuge

The young couple, newlyweds perhaps, wait until the other visitors in the Gilbert's Bar House of Refuge gift shop are far enough away before they turn to the shopkeeper and sheepishly whisper their question.

"Ah," she replies in a stage whisper. She's heard the question many times before. Few folks ask it in front of others. "All the spirits we have here," she says, "are happy ones."

That makes perfect sense, of course. The Gilbert's Bar House of Refuge, at 301 SE McArthur Boulevard on Hutchinson Island, was one of ten such lifesaving stations built along Florida's Atlantic coast in the last half of the nineteenth century, and it was all about saving lives. The houses were strung along the coast at intervals so that no stranded sailor would have to walk too far to find help. The decision to build a house of refuge on the St. Lucie Rocks was made after a ship broke up off Hutchinson Island, a splinter-shaped barrier island, in 1873. The sailors from the wrecked vessel struggled ashore to find there was no food, water, or accommodations available for them.

The house of refuge was constructed in 1876 and provided food, shelter, and canvas cots in the upstairs sleeping quarters for stranded seafarers until 1945, when it was officially closed. Hubert Bessey, the house's sixth keeper, served there from July 1890 to January 1, 1902. He married Susan Corbin, of Nashville, who added a woman's touch to the house and surroundings, making the place even more accommodating and homelike to homesick seafarers.

Originally, the houses of refuge had been created under the jurisdiction of the Department of Treasury, but the passage of Senate Bill 2337 in 1914 and its subsequent signature by President Woodrow Wilson in January 1915 created the United States Coast Guard, which brought together the U.S. Life-Saving Service and the Revenue Cutter Service. The Coast Guard, which operated the houses of refuge, was governed by the Department of Treasury during peacetime and the U.S. Navy during war.

During its years of service, the house provided comfort to the stranded, shipwrecked, and beached crews of vessels small to large, such as the molasses-laden 371-ton brigantine *J. H. Lane* that wrecked five miles south of Gilbert's Bar. Seven crewmen were saved, but one perished.

In 1904, the staff dispatched dories to assist the *George Valentine*, a 767-ton bark from Italy that was stranded offshore. The lifesavers rescued seven of the twelve-member crew. A day later, a Spanish vessel, *Cosme Colzado*, was stranded, and one crewman died as a result.

The U.S. Navy began using the house of refuge in 1941 as a patrol station for the beach. A watch tower was constructed to search for German vessels patrolling offshore.

The boathouse, built in 1914 and lovingly restored in 1976, has been transformed into a museum that shows how the houses of refuge functioned and assisted seafarers. An upstairs dormitory was added after the Coast Guard took over operations. The boathouse is outfitted with period furniture and furnishings, augmented by a display of photographs and other artwork. The building is bright, neat, and well maintained. There's not a cobweb in sight, and no one will lose a moment's sleep after visiting.

The house of refuge, now operated as a museum by the Historical Society of Martin County, does have its otherworldly aspects, though. Beachgoers have reported smelling the scent of Mrs. Bessey's southern favorites cooking when they walk down the beach by the place, even when it is unoccupied. Others have noticed the scent of cigar or aromatic pipe smoke coming from the house. Sometimes folks catch a glimmer of light in the darkened windows at night. But there are no shrieks, no screams, no rattling chains or sudden cold spots. It's always warm at Gilbert's Bar House of Refuge, where the spirits are happy ones indeed.

Antique Ghosts

The aging building that houses the Treasure Coast Antique Mall, on U.S. 1 not far from the Martin County border, was situated to look out over the strip of land between it and the ocean. Built originally as the home for a Bulgarian orchestra director, the six-bedroom home later was pressed into service as an inn, restaurant, and brothel. It also was said to have been used as a watch house for the Germans during the 1940s. Its various incarnations attracted a variety of high-profile clientele. Gloria Swanson is said to have dropped by for dinner, as did Joe Kennedy, who drove up from the family's winter compound on Palm Beach. Mobster Al Capone, who had a home in Miami Beach, allegedly visited often when it served as a brothel. The building now houses an antique mall, where dealers rent booths to sell their antiques and fine collectibles.

The ghostly activity here seems to have originated in the days when it served as the best little bordello in St. Lucie County. The spirit of a customer shot dead on the stairway is said to still inhabit the place, and the manly aroma of cigar smoke sometimes wafts through the bedroom where Capone is said to have slept. It seems that antiques are not the only vestiges of the past that you can find here.

Glossary

Apparition: A disembodied spirit that appears visibly to humans; the sudden or unexpected appearance of persons or objects.

Botanica: Shops specializing in the sale of items of magical or spiritual interest, such as prayer candles, amulets, talismans, herbs, powders, or incense. Many botanicas also carry items used by voodoo or Santeria practitioners.

Ectoplasm: The external layer of cytoplasm within a cell, and the only tangible evidence of ghosts or other spirits. Ghost hunters and other paranormal investigators analyze photographic anomalies to detect ectoplasm as residual evidence of spiritual presence.

Exorcism: A ceremony that serves to banish evil or unwanted spirits from a person, object, or dwelling. The ceremony commonly uses prayers, blessings, and other religious rites to release the spirit from its dwelling place.

Ghost: The disembodied spirit of a deceased being, usually but not always human.

Orbs: Spherical balls of light, long believed by many to be the trapped souls of the departed.

Paranormal: Anything beyond the range of normal human experience or in defiance of accepted scientific explanation.

Poltergeist: Created from the German words *poltern* (to make noise) and *geist* (ghost). A poltergeist is a ghost that causes disturbance through noise, motion, or disarray.

Séance: A gathering of persons who, under the guidance of a medium, communicate with departed persons.

Bibliography

Books and Articles

Achenbach, Joel. "For Sale: Home with Ghost; Historic, Haunted Little Haiti Villa to Be Auctioned Off." *Miami Herald,* May 1, 1985.

Adams, Earl. "Aged Lover's Wife Enters Bizarre Case: Writes from Florida City She's Ready to Talk of Von Cosel." *Miami Herald,* October 10, 1940.

"Aged Key Wester Used 'Body' to Gratify Sex Passion," *Miami Life* 15:6, November 2, 1940.

"Associated Press Checks Mysterious Call about 83-Year-Old Eccentric Karl Tanzler Von Cosel: Still Alive." *Key West Citizen,* August 1, 1952.

Bellamy, Jeanne. "Life Never Departs the Body: So Says Key West's Strangest Lover," *Miami Herald,* c. 1940.

———. "Protests Love of Corpse in 3-Hour Hearing, Jailed." *Miami Herald,* October 8, 1940.

Bethel, Rod. *A Halloween Love Story.* Key West, FL: self-published, 1988.

Borden, Lucie Page. "How Dress Rules the World," *American Eagle* 93:225, Spring 2000.

Bridgwater, Mark. "Old Boston House Haunted by Titillating Tales." *Palm Beach Post,* October 31, 1992.

Buckley, Cara. "Evolution of a Legend." *Miami Herald,* April 19, 2005.

Bucsko, Mike. "Boston House Put on National Register." *Port St. Lucie News,* April 13, 1985.

Capozzi, Joe. "Baseball's Most Famous Haunt," *Palm Beach Post,* May 20, 2007, 6B.

Collins, LeRoy. "The Tale of a Man Obsessed by Time." *St. Petersburg Times.* October 7, 1985.

Coral Castle English Tour Guide. Brochure available at Coral Castle ticket booth, Homestead.

Dauray, Charles. "Back to the Future." *American Eagle* 95:227, Spring 2001.

Davis, Christine. "Scary Stories: Digging Up Tales of Poltergeists and Ghostly Doings." *Sun-Sentinel,* October 30, 1996.

Dodge, Mary. "Boston House Seeks Spot in Register." *Port St. Lucie News,* October 21, 1984.

Dunlop, Beth. "Old Haunts: When It Comes to Architecture, Ghosts Seem to Prefer the Exotic." *Miami Herald,* October 31, 1988.

Edwards, Gina. "Skunk Ape, Celebrity Wedding Make Collier a Tabloid Haven." *Naples Daily News,* December 20, 1997.

Erstein, Hap, Kevin D. Thompson, Gary Schwan, and Charles Passy. "Palm Beach's Haunted Museum! Channel 12's Anchor Shot! The Tornado on Stage!" *Palm Beach Post,* October 29, 1999.

"Gilbert's Bar House of Refuge." Tour pamphlet/information sheet distributed at the site.

Gillis, Chad. "The Koreshan Legacy: Cult's Assets, Legacy Now Split among Three Separate Groups." *Bonita Daily News,* May 13, 2001.

DiPino, David. "Blue Anchor Lures with a Haunted Past, Beers." *West Boca Forum,* December 12, 2007, 41.

———. "The Koreshan Legacy: Koreshan Beliefs Sprang from Idea to Improve Christianity." *Bonita Daily News,* May 13, 2001.

———. "The Koreshan Legacy: Koreshan Building Plans Stir Passions in Estero." *Bonita Daily News,* May 13, 2001.

———. "The Koreshan Legacy: Leader Preached Reincarnation, Communal Living, Celibacy and Equity." *Bonita Daily News,* May 13, 2001.

———. "The Koreshan Legacy: Rich Koreshan History Largely Kept Private." *Bonita Daily News,* May 13, 2001.

Guthrie, John J., Jr., Phillip Charles Lucas, and Gary Monroe, eds. *Cassadaga: The South's Oldest Spiritualist Community.* Gainesville: University Press of Florida, 2000.

Harakas, Margo. "The Legend of Snake Warrior's Island." *Sun-Sentinel,* October 20, 1996.

Harrison, Ben. *Undying Love: The True Story of a Passion That Defied Death.* Far Hills, NJ: New Horizon Press, 1997.

Hartzell, Scott Taylor. "Woman's Fiery Death Remains Worldwide Enigma 51 Years Later." *St. Petersburg Times,* June 12, 2002.

Headrick, Christina. "For Many Sunshine Skyway Bridge Is a Dark Symbol of Sadness and Loss." *St. Petersburg Times,* April 13, 1988.

Hudson, Julie Enders. "Something Spooky on the Second Floor." *Fort Pierce News Tribune,* May 17, 1985.

Bibliography

Jamiolkowski, Tim. "Boston House in FP Is Added to Register of Historic Places." *Fort Pierce News Tribune,* April 14, 1985.

Johnson, Stanley, and Phyllis Shapiro. *Once upon a Time.* Boca Raton, FL: Arvida Corporation, 1987.

Kinney, Henry. *Once upon a Time: The Legend of the Boca Raton Hotel and Club.* Boca Raton, FL: Arvida Corporation, 1966.

Kircher, Ralf. "Dave Shealy: On the Trails of a Skunk Ape." *Naples Daily News,* September 5, 1999.

Kleinberg, Eliot. "Undying Love." *Palm Beach Post,* October 29, 1995.

Klingener, Nancy. "Undying Love: The Bizarre Tale of a Romance that Even Death Could Not End Unfolds in Key West," *Miami Herald,* June 13, 1993.

Koreshan State Historic Site. Pamphlet by Florida Department of Environmental Protection, Division of Recreation and Parks.

The Koreshan Unity Settlement. Self-guided tour pamphlet created by the Koreshan Unity Alliance, Inc., available at the Koreshan State Historic Site, Estero.

Lambert, Clay. "Treasure Coast Boasts of Haunted Houses." *Palm Beach Post,* October 25, 1998.

Lancaster, Cory Jo. "For a Myth, He Sure Looks Big and Smells." *Orlando Sentinel,* August 2, 1992.

Latham, Sally. "Boston House a Stately Monument to History." *Fort Pierce News Tribune,* March 10, 1974.

Leedskalnin, Edward. *A Book in Every Home.* Homestead, FL: self-published, 1936.

Long, Phil. "Stories about Spirits Just Won't Die." *Miami Herald,* October 29, 1995.

Lopez, Lalo. "Media-Fueled Chupacabra-Mania Raises 'Fact or Fiction' Hysteria." *Hispanic* (August 1996), 12–13.

Lorraine, Bill. "Von Cosel's Wife." *Florida Keys Magazine,* October 1982.

Lykins, Lorrie. "Take a Walk on the Weird Side," *St. Petersburg Times,* October 13, 2005.

McIver, Stuart. "King of a Jungle River." *The Florida Chronicles,* vol. 3. Sarasota, FL: Pineapple Press, 2001.

More Boca Legends. Third annual Fiesta de Boca Raton program book, 1966.

Morgan, Curtis. "Favorite Haunts: Ghosts Aren't Shy about Spooking South Florida." *Miami Herald,* July 23, 1999.

Muir, Helen. *The Biltmore: Beacon for Miami.* Miami: Valiant Press, 1998.

Nevins, Buddy. "'Lost Patrol' Is Part of Bermuda Triangle Legend." *Fort Lauderdale News,* May 22, 1983.

Palmore, Mary-Frazier. "Earthbound Spirits in Ft. Pierce?" *Indian River Life,* January 1979.

Partington, Karie. "Koreshan Ghost Walk Offers Realistic Glimpse of Estero's Early Settlers." *Bonita Daily News,* December 29, 2000.

Phillips, Kendall J., and Steve Ziskinder, "The Historic Boston House." *Treasure Coast Prime Times,* October 1999.

"Police Officer Bienvenido Perez Only Living Person Who Knows Where Elena Buried." *Key West Citizen,* August 15, 1952.

Rea, Sara Weber. *The Koreshan Story.* Estero, FL: Guiding Star Publishing House, 1994.

Roat, Paul. "Skyway Disaster, 25 Years Later." [Anna Maria Island, FL] *Islander Reporter,* May 11, 2005.

Schudel, Matt. "Dancing with the Devil Doll." *Sunshine Magazine [Sun-Sentinel]* October 26, 1997.

Smith, Susy. *Ghosts around the House.* Cleveland: World Publishing Co., 1970.

Solomon, Irvin D. "South Florida and the Hollow Earth Experiment." *South Florida History* 27:4, Fall 1999.

Thurwachter, Mary. "Florida's Historic Haunts." *Palm Beach Post,* October 29, 2000.

Traphagen, Mitch. "Finding Florida: Getting into the Spirit of Things." [Ruskin, FL] *Observer News,* August 31, 2006.

Tunstall, Jim, and Cynthia Tunstall. "Spooky Stories Abound in Tampa Area." *USA Today,* October 29, 2003.

Vaughan, Chris. "Site of Former Cuban Consulate May Receive Historic Designation." *Miami Herald,* June 30, 1983.

———. "Taking Measure of History." *Miami Herald,* November 6, 1983.

Welch, Jamie. "Who's Haunting Anderson's Corner?" *South Florida History* 26:4, Fall 1998.

Winsberg, Morton D. *Florida's History through Its Places.* Gainesville FL: University Press of Florida, 1995.

Zucco, Tom. "Hunt for Haunts." *St. Petersburg Times,* October 31, 2002.

Online Sources

"Artist House Key West." www.artisthousekeywest.com/history.htm.

"Cassadaga." www.cassadaga.org/history.htm.

Drizin, Lee. "Treasure Hunt: Discover a Bit of Local History While You Hunt for Collectibles." *Island Life Online,* www.islandlifeonline.com/treasure7_01.shtml.

Bibliography

"Gilbert's Bar House of Refuge, Florida: Coast Guard Station #207." www.uscg.mil/history/STATIONS/GILBERTS%20BAR.html.

"Henry Morrison Flagler biography." www.flaglermuseum.us/html/ flagler_biography.html.

Hinson, Mark. "Haunted Tallahassee." www.tdo.com/features/ stories/0725/.

"Koreshan State Historic Site." www.dep.state.fl.us/parks/district_4/ koreshan/.

Martin, Meg. "Visions of Jack Kerouac." *PointsSouth.* July 1, 2005. www.pointerinstitute.com.

"The Skyway Bridge—Yesterday, Today and Tomorrow." www.dot.state.fl.us/Structures/designConf2006/Presentations/ session20/Final-20Garcia.pdf.

Other Sources

Elliott Museum. Channel 5 News at 11, WPTV-TV, West Palm Beach, October 29, 2003.

Photocopy of personal correspondence from Ruhl Pace to Earl Adams, September 23, 1961.

"Ghosts Hunters of the Space Coast," film, 3 Boys Productions, 2000.

Acknowledgments

To our patient editor, Kyle Weaver, and the helpful staff at Stackpole Books, we offer our deepest appreciation.

Librarians, archivists, and staff from historical organizations throughout the state were kind in answering our endless questions and obtaining information for us. We thank you all. The following people went especially out of their way to assist: Laurin Bosse, director of public relations, Flagler College, St. Augustine; Dr. Terrence A. Cronin Jr., principal, 3 Boys Productions, Melbourne; Charles Dauray, president and CEO, The College of Life Foundation, Estero; Christopher Eck, Denyse Cunningham, Helen Landers and Mary Rose Harding at the Broward County Historical Commission, Fort Lauderdale; Susan Gillis, archivist, Boca Raton Historical Society; Lydia and Tom Hambright, May Hill Russell Library, Key West; Vickie Joslyn, Lake Worth City Library; Beverly Mustaine, Museum of the City of Lake Worth; Merrilyn Rathbun, director of research services, Fort Lauderdale Historical Society; and Elizabeth A. Smith, Florida Geographical Alliance, Florida State University, Tallahassee.

About the Authors

CYNTHIA THUMA IS A FLORIDA NATIVE AND lifelong resident who has lived in Broward and Palm Beach Counties in the southeastern part of the state and Leon County in the north. She is the author of several books on Florida history.

CATHERINE LOWER IS A MICHIGAN NATIVE who has lived in Broward and Miami-Dade Counties in Florida but now makes her home in Murfreesboro, Tennessee, just outside Nashville. She is the editor of a self-help book.

Together, Cynthia and Catherine wrote the book *Creepy Colleges and Haunted Universities*.

Other titles in the
Haunted Series

HAUNTED
GEORGIA
by Alan Brown
978-0-8117-3443-1

HAUNTED MARYLAND
by Ed Okonowicz
978-0-8117-3409-7

HAUNTED TEXAS
by Alan Brown
978-0-8117-3500-1

HAUNTED WEST VIRGINIA
by Patty A. Wilson
978-0-8117-3400-4

WWW.STACKPOLEBOOKS.COM
1-800-732-3669